Written From The Heart

Written From The Heart

Ron Farrow

iUniverse, Inc.
New York Lincoln Shanghai

Written From The Heart

iUniverse, Inc.

For information address:
iUniverse, Inc.
2021 Pine Lake Road, Suite 100
Lincoln, NE 68512
www.iuniverse.com

ISBN: 0-595-30437-0

Printed in the United States of America

For
Marjorie Holmes
and
My wife, Glenda
The two women in my life who
had faith, without doubt, that
this book would become a reality.

Contents

Acknowledgments

My heartfelt thanks to the following:
My daughter, Donna, who spent hours editing my articles,
before their first publication in my newspaper column.
Dana Talley, for taking all my articles and letters,
and with precision making them a manuscript, for this book.
Her guidance and management skills, made a
good book, a great book to read.
My wife, Glenda, who has always been and
still is the wind beneath my wings.

Introduction

Writing articles from the heart reveals what is in the heart of the person who writes them. As I read the articles in this book, I saw the heart of a lover, dreamer, and talented prolific writer. A person in touch with the heart of God. A person in search of a perfect world in a world of un-perfect people. One who looks beyond the obvious and analyzes the hearts and minds of those he comes into contact with.

As he reflects on his past and his life experiences, he releases his pain by sharing it and relives his joy by recalling it. This is a book about life, his life and ours.

Within the pages of this book a precious gift is to be found for those who read them. A legacy of the writers life and the way life was once upon a time.

Dana Talley

1

Lessons a Husband Must Learn

The past 27 years has been a learning experience. I would like to think that I have finally arrived at the graduating ceremony.

With each passing day, I realize this is only wishful thinking, as I daily learn the thing I really know is how little I know. What I do know, however, must be taught by any wife who intends to have a lasting relationship, and must be learned by any husband for the relationship to be a lasting one.

Lesson one: Two things husbands don't mess with.

There are two things a husband shouldn't mess with. This should be taught right away, even before the honeymoon is over. The two things are, "You don't mess with my car" and "You don't mess with my purse." A woman's car is her power symbol and her freedom card.

When behind the wheel, she is in charge to go where she wants and when she wants, for whatever reason, usually to take her to the mall, or some other place she can use those pretty plastic cards in her purse. Which brings me to the second thing: a woman's purse.

My great-grandfather once told me a story of how life was in his youth. He said that he remembered once seeing an Indian get on another man's horse, and when the man came out of the saloon and caught the Indian red-handed, he pulled out his gun and shot him dead.

I remember the first time I decided to take a journey through the pockets of my wife's purse. I had hardly begun my adventure, when out of nowhere, there she stood, looking at me. I felt like that Indian, and my wife looked at me like that man who caught the Indian on his horse. I thought my life was over. This demand for privacy extends beyond the purse. It must include a woman's dresser and drawers where she keeps her clothing; her closet, and any space she deems to be her private space. The purse is a good place to begin this lesson, as this is where a woman can hide sales receipts, lay-away, and "mad money," just to name a few things.

Lesson two: The check book—only God knows.

A man must learn to go beyond being a CPA in keeping up with the correct balance or the reasoning of the irregularities of the checkbook.

If, as many couples do, you pool your money into one checking account and you don't want your husband to be immediately alarmed, there are things a woman has to do.

In the beginning, you can just fail to write the check in the book, cover it with your "mad money" when you can, and don't enter the deposit in the book either. This will teach him to look for missing check numbers and make him more disciplined in opening up those returned checks from the bank. After he has learned this lesson, you can proceed to writing "void" on checks you don't want him to know about—tell him you made a mistake (which is true; however, the mistake was not telling him why you wrote the check) and then find a reason to write an explainable check following the one you just voided.

This will extend his ability to read the statement from the bank and match dollar amounts with check numbers.

After he prides himself in his detective ability of staying on top of the checkbook, there is always more you can do to keep him alert.

The next step would be to always get the mail before he does. This will give you the opportunity to remove any checks you have not entered in the checkbook and remove them or remove the checks you wrote "void" on. This will have him confused for days and will give you time to have a good reason for writing the check, which somehow got lost somewhere. The checkbook is a woman's teaching aid for her husband to be effective in cost management and bookkeeping.

Lesson three: All men suffer from memory loss.

Most men are less than observant of their immediate surroundings, and this includes their wives as the years slip by. Thus, a woman must use some great shock treatment to instill this quality, so much needed by women in general.

A good place to start is with those clothes you have been hiding in the closet. Clothes are never new! After you have worn them a time or three, your husband asks, "Where did that come from?" You look at him as if he has lost it, and tell him you've had it for years (and in your heart, you have). After he tells himself how blind he's been, he will probably apologize, and for a few days at least, take notice of what you are wearing.

This lesson must be repeated frequently, as he will sink once again into his state of nonobservance—a condition that seems to prevail in the male species. As he grows older, you may find it necessary to make the "lessons" more dramatic, perhaps with the use of new furniture or a new car.

Lesson four: You're in charge of the home; He is in charge of the grass that surrounds it.

There are exceptions to every rule, including this one, but for the most part, women have a more refined taste in aesthetics when it comes to home decor.

They also have a fanatical need to move furniture whenever they wish, wherever they wish, and for whatever reason they wish. This is an area men must learn to leave alone and to their wives, unless they are asked to participate. Some men may accept this quite well, others may not.

Women have a third eye that allows them to see how things are and how they are going to be when they get done changing them. Heaven help the man that tries to stand in their way.

This lesson should begin in a gradual way and be increased with time. Moving smaller furniture or lamps, little things you already own is a good start. This should be followed by the purchase of new things, small items at first, but never to match the present decor of your home. Always look to the day when you cover the paneling you despise with beautiful wallpaper that clashes with the carpet. The carpet people will be happy to deliver the new carpet they've been holding for what seems like an eternity. You can then bring in the new furniture you've been paying on for at least two years. This lesson comes slow, but eventually rewards a woman with that elusive contentment she seeks from her environment.

As I continue to record the many lessons I have learned and those that are sure to come, I sincerely hope the four explained in this article have found a place in your heart.

2

Are We Blind to the Greatness of the United States?

During my freshman year of high school, a boys and girls choir from the school for the blind in St. Louis came to give a performance. Prior to their performance, they were standing outside on the school grounds waiting to perform. As I looked at this beautiful group of high school students, I felt so sorry for them. They were a beautiful group of students, but they couldn't behold each other's beauty, not even their own, as they were legally blind.

Their performance began with "This Is My Country." Perhaps you are familiar with the song: "This is my country, land that I love. This is my country, grandest on Earth." When they lifted their beautiful voices to this song, I felt chills sweep through my entire body. Tears came to my eyes. I never had felt so patriotic in my entire life as I felt that day. With no eyes to see this great land, they sang with compassion. It was absolutely awesome.

Only a few weeks ago, my grandson, Elijah, and I were sitting on the steps in front of my house observing the Riverfest fireworks display. Each time a display appeared, I said, "Look, Elijah." He would reply, "Say awesome, Papa." Elijah will not see any fireworks on this Fourth of July. He is in Croatia with his mother, who hopes to minister and bring healing to that land. I have spoken with my daughter only once since their arrival. Nevertheless, as she informed me of the living conditions there, it made me realize just how blessed we are in this great country. Still, it seems most of us are blind to this fact. When compared with many other nations in the world, one can surely say America is an awesome country. Celebrate.

3

Music Groups Praised

I would like to express my appreciation for the excellent performance presented by the symphonic wind ensemble conducted by Robert M. Gifford and the Cape Girardeau Central High School Salsa Project led by Mark Ellison at Academic Auditorium.

Our city is most certainly blessed to have such talented music students and teachers such as Gifford and Ellison.

My entire life has been filled with a love of and appreciation for music. Never have I received so much in one evening as I received from this concert.

My thanks to all who made this possible.

4

Take Me Out to the Fair

It's that time of the year again—time for the local county fairs.

Soon, I will be going to our own SEMO District Fair. I love this time of the year and I love going to the fair. Fair time is always a forecast that cooler weather is around the corner, as I can remember several years when we would have a fire in our fireplace during fair week.

What makes the fair so appealing may vary from one person to another. Some enjoy the animal displays, others love the food. For kids, both young and old, it probably is the rides and the midway. Yes, the rides—rides such as the Ferris wheel.

I have never considered myself to be afraid of heights, until one day while at the county fair. I was 15 years old, and a lady came up to me and asked if I would take her grandson, who was around five years old, on the ferris wheel for her, as she was afraid to ride this ride.

I had been on this ride before, and it seemed pleasant enough, so I agreed to do this for her. When we stopped on the top, as you always do on this ride, the 5-year-old began to swing us back and forth, and tried to climb over the side to say hi to his grandma.

Fear swept over me, and I must have looked as pale as I felt inside, for I was in terror. The fact that we were so far from the ground—and I was responsible for getting this kid back down again in one piece—filled me with terror.

I was recently informed of another situation involving a ferris wheel, which created terror in the heart of a little girl who has been a friend of mine since the day she was born.

This little girl lost her daddy when she was 2-years-old. She was, and still is told, as she will ask often, that daddy was taken, up high in the sky, to be with God in heaven.

Her mother had taken her and her little sister to an amusement park, and her little sister wanted Mommy to take them on the ferris wheel.

Mommy agreed, but my little friend did not want to go on a ride that went so high. So Mommy took her little sister on the ferris wheel and left her behind with a friend.

As she watched her mommy and little sister being taken away on the ferris wheel, she began to cry, and she cried until they returned to her side.

It was not told to me why she cried, or what thoughts were going through her mind. But one must wonder, if the insecure feelings she had been experiencing since she lost her daddy created terror in her heart, as she watched her mommy and little sister being taken away, up high in the sky, just like her daddy had been taken, way up in the sky to be with God.

Years have passed since she lost her daddy, but the fear of losing someone else remains in her little heart. Who would have thought that a ride at an amusement park, designed to create joy and happiness, could create such terror, such as the terror of a ferris wheel?

Yes, there are the rides. And then there's the midway. Yes, the midway, where they try to lure you into their parlors, to win a teddy bear or some other item.

When fair time comes, I am always reminded of a lesson I learned as a child one year when I went to the fair.

I was so happy that year, as I had saved $20 to have a really good time. I had money to ride the rides, and money enough to eat whatever food I found to be appealing—like hot dogs, a burger or cotton candy.

I arrived at the fair early and was waiting for the rides to get started, as they would normally wait for a large crowd before they would run them.

In my wallet, I had my crispy new looking $20 bill, just burning a hole in my pocket. I heard a lot of commotion going on at one of the "games of chance," so having nothing else to do, I went there to see what was happening.

There was a man and a woman laying money on a table. As the person inside spun a wheel, if their money was on the right color, they received twice the amount of money they had placed, in return. I observed them winning money for about five minutes, and then they left.

I wondered why they quit, when they were doubling their money?

The man inside the stand said to me, "Come here, son." I walked over closer to the stand. "Soon," he said, "there are going to be a lot of people coming by, and I need to have a winner here when they do.

"Let me show you how this game is played. Have you got a dollar we can use?"

I told the man I had a $20 bill. He said, "Here, I'll give you change." He gave me change for the twenty, and I handed him back a dollar.

The man then put the dollar on the color I picked and spun the wheel. It landed on my color, and he said, "See, if we were really playing, you would have won $2 back. Would you like to play for real? I need you to tell everybody how you won money at my stand." I said, "Sure."

The man told me to give him $5 and pick a color. I gave him a $5 bill, expecting to win $10, as I picked my favorite color, which was green. He spun the wheel, and it landed on yellow.

The man said, "Sometimes you have to play more than once to win, try again." I gave him the five $1 bills I had, after he broke my twenty, and placed them on green. He spun the wheel again, and it landed on red.

I began to feel depressed, as I once had twenty and now I only had a $10 bill. I said, "I don't think I like this game," and I started to walk away. After all, $10 would at least let me eat and perhaps have one or two rides. The man said, "Look here, kid. If you want to win your $10 back, you only need to place your $10 bill on a color, and when the wheel stops on that color, you will have the twenty you started with."

Oh how I wanted my $20 back. So I placed my last $10 on green, and he spun the wheel. I felt fear sweep over me as it began to come to a stop. It landed on blue. "Sorry, kid," he said, as he put my last $10 in his pocket.

Words cannot describe the sickness and heartache I felt as I left his stand. I had come to the fair happy, with plenty of money to spend. Now, I was at the fair with no money to spend and very mad at myself for being so trusting of someone I had never seen before, nor would I ever see again.

I was so hurt over this event, I refused to go to a fair for the next two years.

I got over the hurt, and I learned a lesson I have never forgotten. From that time on, when I went to the fair, I stayed away from the con stands. I eat first, then take to the rides. Then, if I have a little change left over, I play the cranks, where you attempt to pick up a round washer that says "choice." This game, like everything else, used to be a dime, and now it is about fifty cents.

As I watch the crowds of people flock to the con-stands each year, and lose money in the false hope of winning a prize, I am almost thankful that once upon a time, I went to the fair and had a $20 lesson. Will someone "Take Me Out To The Fair?"

5

Don't Fence Me In

Give me room, lots of room beneath the starry skies above. So goes the song "Don't fence me in." This song should be every cigarette smokers' theme song.

Beneath the starry skies above is about the only place left a smoker can enjoy this vice and perhaps the last straw of independence that broke the camels "pack," I mean back. I know they are saying "warning smoking is hazardous to your health". I know that morning, noon and night you can hear the cry "second hand smoke has been determined to be hazardous to one's health—even the unborn fetus".

Today's thinking is something like this. It is wrong for someone to blow nicotine into the unborn fetus, but a woman has the right if she wants to take the baby's life before the baby is born. Why the cry about second hand smoke? What or who is making all this noise and stirring everyone into a frenzy about people who want to smoke? Smoking is not wrong if it's just killing you. It's wrong if it is killing you and me. This is the thinking of the world today. A person can eat themselves to their grave. But your overeating will not send me to my grave. It is a matter of survival. The world is telling homosexuals, it is ok to be that way, but if you have AIDs, please stay away. The train of thought is not a concern for others, it is a fearful concern for ourselves. So if you must smoke, don't smoke at your work place, in your home with nonsmokers or on your church parking lot. Smoke out there with the eighteen wheelers, trains, planes, and automobiles under the starry skies above.

Go blow smoke on your tulips, find a butterfly or ladybug and give them a lung full. Let the birds and the bees, the plants, and the trees absorb your carbon monoxide and nicotine. After all, they don't have rights, do they?

It is a real dilemma. Both sides saying "Don't Fence Me In." Our planet is becoming a small, small world with an increasing population. Likes and dislikes must find a place to meet.

When the motive becomes a true concern for the other person instead of a fearful concern for ourselves, we will be more considerate and kind and stop putting up trespass signs all around us when others have not learned or reached that stage in life where a healthy environment is on top of their priority list.

Until then—Don't Fence Me In.

6

Tips for the Motorists in Summer Heat

As it was in the summer of 1996, I once again find myself driving a car without an air conditioner. In May of this year, I replaced the Freon, which I lost last summer, and had a dye added to my Freon so that if I lost it again this year the dye would show under a black light where my Freon leaked out. Thus the problem would be solved forever, right?

In six weeks my Freon was completely depleted. And the dye? No trace of it could be found with the black light. In light of this, and in speaking with so many others who have found themselves without air conditioning this year, I offer some tips on survival while driving a car without an air conditioner:

- Avoid driving between 9 a.m. and 8 p.m. Nevertheless, if you must, the following shall apply:

- Remember that 3 p.m. is suicide hour, which has no resemblance to happy hour, I might add.

- Keep windows down while driving. Your hair will survive. So what if the dog jumps out of the car.

- Do not leave foodstuff in the car, unless you're preparing it on the car dash for your evening meal. I should mention that doing this will save you money and will avoid heating up the kitchen with your range.

- Limit the passenger load to no more than two people. This helps avoid additional body heat and unpleasant odors. You know what I mean.

- Do not smoke while driving. It will be hard enough to breath as it is.

• Plan your trips in advance. There is no such thing as joyriding in a car that isn't air conditioned.

In conclusion, just use good common sense. And remember these words by Henry David Thoreau: "It is not worthwhile to go 'round the world to count the cats in Zanzibar."

7

Marching to the Beat of a Different Drum, Dancing to the Rhythm of a Song

The birth of this article began as I sat listening to my son. He was playing drums by tapping his feet, and hand slapping his knees, to the rhythm of one of his pieces of music from marching band. Without questioning how he would ever find the money for such events, he was voicing his dreams, his goals, and all the things he wanted to buy for his drum set.

During a pause in his conversation, I said, "Ronald, you are marching to the beat of a different drum." He looked at me like, "OK, is this a trick statement?" When he saw I was serious, he asked, "What did you just say?"

"You're marching to the beat of a different drum. Dancing to the rhythm of a different song." I could tell by his expression he was still confused, so we discussed how wonderful it is to be young and have dreams, compared to being down in the valley and over the hill, and wondering how the bills will be paid.

One thing was certain, we had reached a point where we were living on two separate levels of thinking and setting priorities.

This life situation with my son was really nothing new, as it existed when I was his age. I found myself confirming this almost daily. When my son complained about being chauffeured to school by Mom, instead of getting to drive the one and only car I own, I would tell him how I used to get up thirty minutes early, to walk two long blocks, to wait for a ride, on an overloaded school bus. Then I would remind him when I complained at his age, about the school bus thing—how my dad would tell me how he got up before the sun, milked all the cows, and then walked for miles, in the snow, all up hill, to get to school.

When my son expressed that $3 a day wasn't enough lunch money, I quickly responded with how I took peanut butter and jelly sandwiches every day in a little brown sack.

My dad, he probably never got to eat lunch until he got home from school. By then, the day was now night from that long walk home, in the snow, and it was time for his evening meal. As it was for me and my dad, so it was for me and my son. We were "Marching to the beat of a different drum", and "Dancing to the rhythm of a different song."

Speaking of dancing, I've noticed this same occurrence with my grandson Elijah. Only recently, however, as it was not true when he was about two months old.

Everything we did together was special, but the thing we enjoyed most was dancing to music. Most of the time we danced to a tape by the Lettermen, or a CD by the Everly Brothers, music from Papa's time. What became an every-night event, began as an occasional pastime, when I would be asked to baby-sit.

Whenever he would fight going to sleep, or lose his temper waiting for his bottle, "With no dance to dance, and no joy too unconfined," I would boldly step in and say, "On with the dance, let joy be unconfined."

He let me hold him and dance with him anyway I wished, as every move I made was his move. We danced as one. Not anymore. Now we are "Dancing to the rhythm of a different song." Elijah is a year and a half old now and dances on his own, in ways I cannot even imitate. Often when I want to dance, he wants to show me how he can turn the music off, and on, off, and on, loud and soft, loud and soft, you get the drift.

Once we were together, on the same planet. Now he is a 18-month-old trying to be a 5-year-old, and living on a different time clock than I. We are "Dancing to the rhythm of a different song," "Marching to the beat of a different drum."

Should I bring my wife into this article? Why not. We have been married for 28 wonderful years, but we definitely "March to the beat of a different drum." She likes to look for bargains, such as 24 rolls of toilet paper for $5.99, six boxes of tissue paper for $5.95, and any other sale on soap. Hand soap, bar soap, dish soap, if it's soap, and on sale, she will buy it. Not one of each, but at least two and sometimes three, so we don't run out. My thinking, is something like this: Hang onto that money, and run on as little paper products and soap as you can. Why have all those dollars been sitting on a shelf in the form of soap and paper, when I can run out and get it when we need it, for about the same price, sometimes for less?

So what, if once in a while someone say's, "We're out of toilet paper?" And I rush to the store to buy a roll or two. No harm done. A little extra time in the rest room never hurt anyone.

While I'm on this soap box, I might also add, we "Dance to the rhythm of a different song" as to how clothes should be laundered.

She likes to separate them out by color and items, and wash all these little bits in piles she has separated. Each little group gets the same amount of soap and water. No wonder she likes to buy all that soap, the way she washes clothes.

She dries them the same way. When she was in the hospital for a stay, I dumped the whole mess in at one time, as full as the washer would hold it. They came out all right! I put them in the dryer, mixed and matched, they all looked the same to me. Think of the water I saved, better yet, think of all the soap I saved!

I let her have her way, but I'm more than amused as to how we can see things in such a different light. This is another "March" we do. I can't see the reason for four light bulbs, in every light fixture, of every room. As long as we can see OK, I see nothing, I mean nothing wrong with having some light bulbs burned out, just hanging in there so the ceiling fans won't look empty. She would rather have four 40-watt bulbs, than two 100-watt bulbs. Now let me ask you, which do you think gives out the most light? She sees things in a different light than I do, that's for sure.

Even though we "Dance to the rhythm of a different song", we dance well together. With our son playing drums in marching band again this year, we will probably try to see and hear him as often as we can, "Marching to the beat, of a different drum."

8

Was Young Steve Mosley Abducted?

I have noticed Steve Mosley's interest in UFOs and aliens. One must wonder why Steve has taken the time to write two letters concerning this issue. Knowing that his wife may send him to another planet for getting back in the letter-writing mode, this must be a subject close to Steve's heart or something similar.

I have been trying to figure out what it is that makes Steve so interested in UFOs. Something from his childhood perhaps? Could it be that a space ship landed in Arena Park one evening while Steve was practicing wiffle ball and the aliens took him away for a while and did something to his head? After all, how can anyone have his sense of humor and be from this planet? I say that as a compliment. I think Steve is one of the most humorous writers I have ever had the pleasure of working with.

Steve might not even be aware that this abduction ever took place. The aliens probably showed him some scary pictures of some really wild things, and these appear in his mind every time he is about to remember his abduction. Wow! I never realized before how messed up Steve is.

If you happen to run into Steve some place, just act normal. We don't want to scare him or anything. Do we?

9

Clinton Turns Woes into Shadows

A shadow: Something that's not there, something that's not real. When light is placed upon it, it goes away.

Kenneth Starr has been after Bill Clinton like a dog chasing a rabbit. I, like many others, have been amazed by the fact that this rabbit has been able to elude this old dog for so long a time.

I think the answer is in the rabbit's ability to cast shadows. The rabbit has turned every gain the dog has made into an elusive image, a shadow. He has been able to cast shadows every time the dog announced he had a scent of wrongdoing, making each new discovery seem vague, dim and unsubstantial.

True, the rabbit has obviously done some shadow casting, making him questionable as to his honesty or loyalty, and he appears to be a dubious creature. Still, one must stand in awe of his ability to create a screen in view of everything that has been brought to light. And by intercepting the rays of truth and by casting shadows, he has made the truth look dim in the light of everything else.

Now it seems the dog has the rabbit by the throat and it's just a matter of time for the rabbit's doom. However, I wouldn't run to the kitchen for a plate to put the rabbit on if I were you. He is a master at creating shadows, and a shadow is something that's not there, something that's not real, and when light is placed upon it, it goes away.

10

Give Thanks for Your Trials and Tribulations

It's that time of the year, when we start thinking about all the things we have to be thankful for. A time when we reflect on the blessings we have received, and include them in our prayers before partaking of that Thanksgiving feast.

I've come to realize, what I suspect many overlook. Our greatest blessings, are the trials and tribulations we experience in our lives. I am learning, "If you're not hurting, you're not growing."

As for myself, my greatest growth need has been patience and endurance. The lack of these traits has caused me much pain. Only a few months ago I had to take up my cross of these trials of endurance in a doctor's office.

The Doctor's Appointment

You have a doctor's appointment. You leave to get there early. The doctor must not wait. You must be there when your name is called. They can't find you in the appointment book, and you become a salesman, convincing them you're in there somewhere.

Finally, they find your name, and ask you to sit down. You've done well, only minutes until your appointment time. Your eyes observe the second hand on your time piece as it rolls by your appointed time.

Your ear becomes familiar with the voice calling out names of patients to see your doctor. Four of them thus far. You feel a desire to relieve yourself of several cups of coffee. You restrain, as the doctor may hand you one of those little cups. You keep glancing at the magazine rack. With only two people left in the waiting room, you tell yourself there's not time.

Forty five minutes have past, and more people are coming in for an appointment to see your doctor. You remain calm, until they are called to see your doctor while you're still waiting.

With a limit on waiting time, seeming more than justified by now, you ask how much longer will it be. They advise you that as soon as the ambulance arrives to take one of the patients out of a room in your doctor's area, you will be next.

You fearfully sit down, wondering next for what. After becoming longtime friends with most everyone in the waiting room, you hear your name.

Your heart, which is beating faster from this long-awaited moment, is quickly monitored with something tightly wrapped around your arm. You are then asked questions you can't answer, because they have inserted a plastic thermometer in your mouth. They ask you to sit half naked on a paper-covered bed, and to wait for the doctor to see you.

In front of you is a dresser, with a mirror that reveals your half-dressed body. Finding this less than entertaining, you look around the room. You begin to visualize what the doctor does with those tubes of jelly and metallic tools. Feeling an urgency to exit the room, your mind is put to rest by the "Doctors Prayer" plaque hanging on the wall.

You faintly hear voices in an adjoining room. You struggle to hear what is being said, as if it is going to determine your condition. You hear someone removing the clipboard off the door of your room. This is it, you think, as you try to look as perfect as possible.

The doctor comes in with an attitude of "You have two seconds to tell me what your problem is, don't waste it!" You have had two hours to prepare for this and your rehearsal is put to the test. The doctor repeats back to you what you just told him and has diagnosed your illness.

He hands you your chart, which now also has an amount you are to pay for this service he provided. Also there is a date in which you are to return.

Return for none other than your next "Doctors Appointment."

There was a time in my life when I would have called this a very painful event. Learning what to do with the pain was my growing experience. By looking at it in a humorous way, and writing about something we have all shared at sometime or another, I can replace the pain with something of value.

There's great strength born of suffering, rewarded by a new strength. Souls must grow, and it's a magical thing to observe this in the lives of others. This recently happened in my presence, having dinner with my wife.

The Couple in the Fast Food Restaurant

They were sitting in the next booth, side-by-side facing me. A young couple in their thirties, I would have guessed. They appeared to be waiting for a part of their meal, as my wife and I were. My wife always wants her sandwiches plain, and this means waiting for it.

While waiting for our food, I kept feeling compelled to look at this couple, sitting so close together, as my wife and I have done in the past, and still do, but not often enough.

It was not their closeness, however, that got my attention. It was the pictures of emotion I was observing on their faces. His face portrayed depression, and radiated hopeless feelings, that would have made a clown cry. I have never seen a face that said more clearly, "I'm a person living in a wretched state of mind."

My heart went out to this man, not having the slightest hint as to why he looked and felt this way.

Their food was served, and I, still waiting on my food, continued to look their way. I turned my eyes away every so often, not wanting to appear to be intruding, while feeling a strong desire to do so.

They let the food sit as they continued in what appeared to be a serious conversation. They spoke in a very low tone, which I could not discern, his head constantly hanging in a downward position.

Her face was one of concern. Concern for whatever conflict in life, I suppose, that had sent him into such a sad state of being.

She listened to him, as if every word was a matter of their greatest importance. As she finally reached down to pick up her sandwich, with hands that were trembling, I witnessed tears coming to her eyes, as she continued wiping them with the same hand that was opening the wrapper. She sat her meal back down on the table, and began talking to him seemingly in a more positive fashion.

By now I was beginning to achieve the art of reading their lips, as I tried to read their minds. Their faces slowly grew closer together, and I saw her smile and heard her whisper to him, "That's not going to happen, do you know why?" He looked up at her and said, "Why?" She smiled and said, "Because I'm not going to let it happen."

With that being said, they both smiled and continued to eat.

Whatever the intruder of life, was, that had put this couple's ability to overcome, on trial, my bet would be she didn't let it happen. Is life, not a wonderful, beautiful thing?

Trials and Tribulations hurt, yet problems and pain, conflicts and disappoint-ment, defeat and tragedies, are essential to one's growth. For every hurt there's a lesson to learn. Hurting teaches us to forgive, hurting teaches us to have compas-sion, hurting teaches us to accept the unacceptable.

One must outgrow the tears and the self pity. One must forsake giving in and nourishing their hurt.

One of the most common and almost certain trials that hurt is the hurt of sep-aration. A broken relationship, the death of a loved one, a child leaves home. The loneliness it brings, and the emptiness. How does one define:

"The Emptiness of an Empty Nest?"

To call a child for breakfast, and get no response. To fling open the door to an empty room. A room with things like books, music tapes and discs, posters, a baseball bat, and outgrown clothes. Things that used to make a child happy until they decided they were no longer children. And they need these items no more.

How does one define the emptiness of an empty nest? The day will come, as sure as death and taxes, the child will leave home, and leave emptiness behind.

When a child leaves home, there prevails a feeling of fantasy, or perhaps false hope. A desire to believe that their leaving is only a temporary thing. One thinks surely they will discover the error of their ways and come running home. Some-times this is the case, but definitely not the rule.

And where this is not the case, one learns how many years a night can last.

The telephone would become your best and closest companion if it would only ring. For it will seem more like a silent partner than a friend. And as the days turn into weeks, and the weeks into months, your imagination becomes your worst enemy.

Creating thoughts of every evil and wrong that could happen to your child. Without faith, fear would overcome you and it seems that faith is all you have to cling to.

Perhaps there are still some children living at home to comfort you. The nest is not totally empty. But now you realize they are not eternal possessions for you to keep. Now they are a constant reminder of the inevitable of what you know will happen.

"Like precious jewels, Vanishing form your treasure chest, One by one." How does one define the emptiness of an empty nest?"

May each and everyone have a blessed Thanksgiving, and remember if you're not hurting your not growing. And give thanks for your trials and tribulations!

11

Encouraging Words are Appreciated

On Aug.7 I received, to my surprise, a card in the mail from Steve Mosley with some wonderful words of encouragement. To receive such encouragement from a writer whom I have so much respect for certainly made my day.

On Aug. 8 a friend gave me the May 1998 issue of Guideposts magazine to read. To my delight I found an article by Jean Bell Mosley, "More Than I Bargained for." It is a wonderful story about her childhood when she was in the fifth grade. We are so fortunate to have an author such as Jean Bell Mosley as a resident of our city.

Then on Aug. 9, while still in a state of euphoria from these two past events, I read Jean Bell Mosley's "For most of the century" serialization in the Southeast Missourian. What a thrill it was to read about her invitation to the annual Guideposts workshop at Rye, N.Y. I felt like I was there with her as I read her wonderful account of the trip and the workshop.

Thinking life could not get better than this, toward the end of her column I was thunderstruck upon reading her story about her encounter with my dear friend, Marjorie Holmes. Jean had related the story to me once before in a letter she sent me. In fact, I think I'm going to stop writing now and see if I can find that letter. It certainly was one of the most treasured things I ever received.

12

Freedom is a Choice

I read with great interest Jack Stapleton's column, "Voter turnout: Is democracy disappearing?" In it he writes, referring to electoral participation, "The democratic system of our forefathers has slowly eroded over the years." After a comprehensive report on numbers, indicating a lack of voter participation, he concludes that the four out of five voters who didn't go to the polls said the issues weren't important. He then concluded, "When freedoms are no longer viewed as important, they cease to exist. Is that what our country is coming to?"

I had just completed writing a column for publication the day before which may add some light to his conclusions. The title of my column was "A misconception of misconduct." An excerpt"

"I think there is a virus that is eating away at the social fabric of what was once a great society, changing the perception of the moral values within that society, a virus infecting our educational, political and social arena by neutralizing the concept of being able to distinguish between right and wrong. It removes the point of view, teaching of and principles of right or wrong. Thus, the function of moral theology will cease to exist. I further believe this virus now has America lying on its back heading for sudden death. It is a virus that says right is wrong and wrong is right until black and white, through blending, become such a gray area we are no longer able to distinguish right from wrong. This virus is called 'Misconception of misconduct.'"

In conclusion, freedom is a choice. When we can no longer detect the black and white line in an issue nor see the choice, it is no longer a freedom. This is what our country is coming to.

13

Looking at My Life Through a Stained Glass Window

The happiest moments I remember from my childhood are the holidays and birthdays. Mom and Dad always made a super effort to make them special and Christmas was no exception.

Beneath the Christmas tree were treats such as apples and oranges and a variety of nuts, pecans, and walnuts. Mom would let us kids decorate the tree—it was great! We strung popcorn with what we didn't eat while performing this enjoyable task.

When people have fond memories such as these, they tend to carry on the traditions they once enjoyed. I have made an effort to make holidays special, golden memory days, for my children.

With Christmas approaching, I have been thinking and reminiscing about the good old days, when I was a child, and when Santa Claus was alive and real. Thinking not so much about past Christmas times I have enjoyed, but how my childhood life was shaped and developed by precious people who took an interest in me.

Holding a Christmas ornament that looked like a stained glass window really made this hit home. Why? Because stained glass is colored by the additions of pigments, a substance that imparts color.

Thus, I began to look at my life, at my past, through a stain glass window. For me to see and understand my true colors, my real nature and beliefs, I would need to look at the people who did the coloring. It was these colorful people and their kindness that has kept my personality from being a colorless pane of glass. Permit me to let you share a view or two through the "stained glass window of my life."

"A Friend and Some Yellow Paint"

"Paper! Get your morning paper, Post and Globe!" These were the words that I shouted as I pushed the large wooden cart, with heavy metal wheels, through the snow. I was very small for an 8-year-old, and would stop and rest now and then, in hopes that someone would step out their door, and ask me to bring them a paper.

The papers were very thick and large, and this made the cart even heavier. However, I was determined to succeed in this business, and get one of those street corners, where you just stood there and waited for a car to pull up and roll down their window.

This came about after a year of pushing the cart. I had the corner of Sprigg and Independence, across from Grace Methodist Church. Cars were driving up every five minutes asking for one and sometimes two papers. Suddenly, something tragic happened. Cars began parking all around my corner, as the car's occupants were attending church. No longer could cars drive up to my corner and roll down their window to buy a paper while the other traffic drove by. Now, if they stopped for me to bring a paper to their car, I was holding up traffic.

My business was beginning to dry up. How could I ever get my prosperous corner back? I remembered seeing a few places where yellow paint had been put on the curb to indicate it was a "NO PARKING ZONE."

If only I could get yellow paint around my corner, this would solve my problem.

I lived in a two-story frame house on the same block where a funeral home was located. Walter, the owner, was not only my neighbor, he was my friend and mayor of the city at that time. "Yes, that is what I will do," I said to myself, "I will go see Mr. Mayor, my friend Walter."

I walked right into the funeral home and asked to see him. They instructed me to enter a room where he had an office. There he sat behind the largest desk I had ever seen in my life.

"Sit down," he said, "How can I help my little friend today." I explained my problem, and offered what I thought would be the solution. Then I waited nervously for his response. He smiled at me and said, "Yes, I see the problem you are having." He continued, "I have been concerned about these cars blocking the visibility at that intersection myself." He rose from his chair, reached out his hand to shake mine and said, "I can't promise anything today, but I will see what I can do." I thanked him and left, with hope in my heart that my friend would help me, and feeling a bit proud that I could talk to the Mayor of Cape Girardeau, just like any adult could come to him with a problem.

The following Sunday, when I arrived at my corner, it was painted bright yellow, all the way around. I learned that no problem is too small or too large to fix, if you have "a friend and some yellow paint."

I was learning a lot for an 8-year-old. I learned if one is willing to start at the bottom, he or she can reach the top. I learned that problems are really opportunities in disguise. I learned the power of City Hall, and more importantly the power of having a friend. The man who gave me that newspaper job taught me another lesson—"where there's a will, there's a way." His name was Mr. Strom. He owned a book store on Broadway. Here is another view I'd like to share with you through the stained glass window of my life.

"Cherry Pink and Apple Blossom White"

The book store was sure bringing back some memories. Mr. Strom the owner, was such a nice man. As a child, I enjoyed window shopping in his store. He had many nice things besides books, under a glass show case. One of the things that caught my eye, was a shiny harmonica. It was so beautiful, and I wanted it so badly. I had never had a harmonica of my own, but my dad had one, and I had blown into it a few times. Mr. Strom was used to me coming in to look at the harmonica, and he would say as I walked in the door, "Yes, it is still here."

There was a hit song being played on the radio, called "Cherry Pink and Apple Blossom White." It was an instrumental song, played on a harmonica. I knew I could learn to play it, if only I could get that harmonica. I had played a "Juice harp" before (at least I think that's what it was called) and I had sore lips for weeks after playing it. I wanted to play this harmonica, and bad.

One day the owner, Mr. Strom said, "How would you like to own this harmonica?" I felt hope leap in my heart as I said, "Really?"

He took the harmonica out of the glass case, and handed it to me. It was the first time I had ever held the harmonica, and it was much heavier than I thought it to be. "I want you to take this harmonica, and go up and down Broadway," said Mr. Strom. "Go into the stores, and tell them you are trying to raise money for this harmonica. Tell them I sent you, play them a song, and bring me back the money you collect."

I was so excited.

Harmonica in hand, I quickly walked out of the store to the sidewalk in front of the store next door. I was afraid that if Mr. Strom could see me, he might change his mind and ask me to give the harmonica back. I set the harmonica on my lips, and attempted to play "Cherry Pink and Apple Blossom White." I was amazed I was able to play it, I could play it just like the recording that was being aired on the radio. Up and down Broadway I went, in and out of the stores, telling my story and playing my song, collecting the change that they put in my hand for Mr. Strom so I could have this harmonica.

I returned to the book store, and showed Mr. Strom the amount of money I had collected. He spread the dimes and nickels over the glass, on top of the showcase where the harmonica once laid, and began counting it. Would there be enough? Would he send me out again or have me come back another day? With fear in my voice and a fainting heart, I worked up the courage to ask, "How much more do I need?"

Mr. Strom smiled a big smile, looked down at me and then said, "If you will play a song for me, I think that will about do it."

I placed the harmonica to my lips and made that final payment, with "Cherry Pink and Apple Blossom White."

The wonderful thing about the stain glass window of one's life, is the coloring process continues. Even now, my life is being influenced by beautiful people who care. One of these people is author "Marjorie Holmes." It was her book "Writing Articles From The Heart" that inspired me to write a column entitled "Written From The Heart."

It has been her continued friendship and support that has strengthened me in the face of defeat and rejoiced with me in my success. Marjorie Holmes lives in Manassas Virginia.

14

I Start Each Day with a Newspaper

On March 17th, I renewed my addiction with the Southeast Missourian. I don't know how I managed to survive so long without it. Every morning I start with the newspaper, pour myself a cup of coffee, and enjoy the first 30 minutes of my day.

Thanks for not just providing a newspaper each day, but a good newspaper with all the local news happenings I may not hear about on radio and TV.

15

Prayer is a Good Addition

I commend the Southeast Missourian for the recent addition of Today's Prayer on the Opinion page. I also fully agreed with the April 19 editorial concerning this addition. I have always been proud of the quality of this newspaper, and this recent decision certainly increased my faith and confidence in those who work hard to make it the best newspaper it can be.

From a humble child of God who is on speaking terms with him, my prayer will be that this newspaper will be blessed for honoring the only one who can give hope and victory in every situation.

16

Bringing in the New Year with Old Expressions (and Some New Strange Terms)

Have you ever gotten up on the wrong side of the bed, looked outside and it was raining cats and dogs, gone to someone and let the cat out of the bag, that your perception of them was they have bats in their belfry, because they were always getting your goat, and making you so mad that this was the last straw that broke the camel's back, and before going to bed, you knocked on wood that tomorrow would be a better day?

What did I just say?

Old expressions and superstitions have found their way into our vocabulary. We find ourselves using these terms handed down by Mom and Dad, or Grandma and Grandpa, knowing not why we use them or where they came from.

A few years ago, I received an anonymous document that gave the source of the above terms, and explained how they came to be used in our vocabulary. I also recently received information from an article in the Dallas Daily news, on some new strange terms invading our speech, according to a university professor. I would like to share this information with you. So if your young'uns should ask you, "What's that supposed to mean?" being the wise all-knowing person you are, you will be able to quickly give them a reply. Additionally we must stay informed as to these new terms, lest our grandchildren speak a language we know not.

We shall begin with, "To get up on the wrong side of the bed." This is believed to doom a person to a day of bad luck and a bad temper. This originates from the superstition, that the left side is the "bad" side. So, getting out of bed on the left, or "wrong" side, is said to be unlucky.

Next was "raining cats and dogs." This is a very old expression. Ancient Norse myths held that cats were able to influence the weather and that the dog was a symbol of the wind. So, "raining casts and dogs" came to be associated with severe rainstorms.

To let the cat out of the bag, is to reveal a secret. The saying goes back to olden times in England, when crooked merchants would put a cat in a sack, and then tell buyers it was a pig. When the buyers got home, they would "let the cat out of the bag" and discover that they had been cheated.

I must confess this next one is one I have never used, nor have heard to any extent. I do like it, however, since I have discovered its reference. To "have bats in one's belfry" is sometimes used to describe a person who is slightly bonkers. It is thought to refer to bats that inhabit a belfry or bell tower. When the bell sounds, the bats fly around wildly, just as peculiar ideas might fly around in a deranged person's mind.

How about "to get one's goat?" This means to annoy or irritate someone. The saying often refers to sneaky practices at the racetrack. Goats often were kept in the stalls with high-strung race horses, to keep the horses calm. If a goat was removed from a stall, the horse would become agitated and would not race well, which was quite annoying for everyone who bet on that particular horse.

Up next, "the straw that broke the camel's back," an expression first used by Charles Dickens in 1848; "The last straw breaks the laden camel's back." It refers to the idea that although camels can carry enormous weights, even the strongest eventually will collapse if it is overburdened. This idea often is applied to humans, as well.

The one I use the most is "to knock on wood." To knock on wood is a super-stition that has persisted for ages. In olden times, trees were believed to harbor protective Spirits. To rap on a tree was to call up the friendly spirit that lived there. It was believed, that this spirit then would protect one against impending bad luck.

We seem to keep certain expressions on tap for special occasions, when we want to make ourselves very understood. Yet many of our best-loved idioms, are shrouded in allusions to long-forgotten customs, or obscured in a fog of etymo-logical absurdities. A few more for your education enjoyment.

- "Paying through the nose": A term we use when we feel we're paying too much. It is related to county noses, and goes back to a Swedish poll-tax which was at one time called a "nose-tax."

- "Looking a gift horse in the mouth": Seeing the worth or value of an idea or opportunity. This dates back to early Roman times. Then as now, the value of a horse was in direct proportion to its age, which could be calculated by look-ing at the condition of its teeth.

- "No ax to grind": The allusion is to a tale attributed to Ben Franklin, about a stranger who so flatters the skill of a boy laboring at a grindstone, that the boy gladly sharpens the stranger's ax for him, presumably for free.

- "To bring home the bacon": This expression originated in the village of Dun-mow, in 11th century England. A side of bacon was offered as a prize to any Englishman who, kneeling on the stones in front of the church door, could swear that for a year and a day, he and his wife hadn't had a single spat, and furthermore he not so much as wished themselves unmarried. Are you think-ing that was a prize never awarded? I would have. It was awarded on eight dif-ferent occasions—all in the short span of 500 years!

- "Can't hold a candle to another": The origin of this phrase, as you might expect antedates the work of Thomas Edison. It was, after all, the candle that illuminated the dark long before electricity was harnessed. Now, holding a smelly, dripping, tallow candle so that someone else could play cards or find their way to the privy was such an unpleasant duty, that it was usually assigned to the most menial of servants. So if someone was said to be unfit to hold a candle for (or to) another, you can be sure that he must have been standing at the very bottom of the ladder in someone else's eyes.

- "To eat humble pie": An extremely distasteful, and perhaps deserved act of being humbled. Humbled pie, used to be humble pie with no h. Saxon ser-vants in merry olde England, used to eat a dish made out of umbels or entrails—the heart, liver and gizzard—of a deer. Yuck! Their Norman masters dined on the good cuts of venison.

- "To get bugged": Have you ever told your kids, "sleep tight, don't let the bed-bugs bite?' Listen to this story: About 50 years ago, an Englishman named Bugged got so bugged by the lowly association of his name with the word of an insect (which to make matters worse, in England referred specifically to the bedbug), that he had his name officially changed to the distinguished and noble name of Norfolk—Howard. This impressed his fellow countrymen so much that they immediately stopped calling bedbugs bugs. From that time on, they were referred to, as "Norfolk-Howards." So the next time your kids or grand-kids go to bed tell them, "Don't let the Norfolk-Howards bite!"

I promised some new terms, but must do it quickly, so I am going to talk fast. "Poorly buffered precipitation" is acid rain, "outside aerial technician" is a telephone lineman, "the non-goal-oriented" are homeless, and "after-sales services" are kickbacks.

Others, "correctional facilities" are prisons. Two for solitary confinement: "involuntary administration separation" and an "individual behavior adjustment unit." "Hemp activism" is trying to legalize marijuana and "clothing-optional lifestyle" is for nudism.

One must wonder what this year will bring, in new language and terms. Topless women now insist on being called "top free," just as "child-free" replaced "childless" among those who don't want children or can't have them.

Recently, I have been hearing myself say, "Ain't that a cats meow?" I still don't have an inkling as to where this term comes from. If you know, perhaps you would be kind enough to write me, so I will be informed as to its original meaning and source. For now, however, I'm going to sit down and write all my new Years resolutions. I already have a few I can share with you.

I will never write an article in 1996, about "underwear in drawers," or about how short I am. I will never tell teachers in an article, "They might be forced to enter the work place."

With this being said, I had better quit, less I wind up, "eating crow." I wish you: "The happiest new year ever" and "May the luck of the Irish be with you in whatever you do." Now I wonder where that comes from?

17

Life's Portraits, Sketches in Time

A photograph of someone who has since passed away. A recording of someone's voice now silenced by the stillness of death's sting. Beneath the soil their bodies lie, yet their presence is ever so with us. The writings of an author. Film clips of an actor. Musical notes written by a famed composer. The painting of an artist. The tools of a carpenter. The beauty once created by skillful hands still amongst us.

These are life's portraits, giving us a sketch in time.

18

Mom Left Memories in Shoe Box

A few years ago my mom gave me an old shoe box filled with memos from my childhood she wanted me to have. Inside the box were photos of me as a child, pictures of various animals I had for pets and other little trinkets and things I had given her over the years. The shoe box contained memories of practically my entire childhood. I have rummaged through that old shoe box many times and could almost tell you every item inside without removing the lid.

My mom recently passed away. As Mother's Day approaches, I wanted so much to write a letter about this special day. However, I just couldn't find the right words to say. In a final effort, I sat at the table and meditated for an idea when suddenly I felt compelled to open up that old shoe box again.

As I removed the lid, I noticed something was written on the underneath side of the lid that I had never seen before. It was my mom's handwriting, and it said, "The flower was my Mother's Day present the first Mother's Day when we lived at 930 N. Middle St."

I had seen the flower she was speaking of many times, and I always wondered why mom gave me an old plastic purple orchid with two plastic leaves of green. I will most likely never remember the present I gave my mom that day. Nevertheless, my mom wanted to make certain that I remember something which meant so much to her: a plastic purple orchid with two plastic leaves of green.

19

Stories that Touch the Heart

As a writer of articles from the heart, this should be my bright and shining month. Hearts everywhere—on cards, boxes of candy, vases of flowers, teddy bears, and anything else that one can use to express their affection for someone they love. Thus, it only seems proper for me to send you my valentine by sharing some of my favorite "heart" stories. Valentine's Day has been one of my favorite days, since I was old enough to know my Dad needed to remember it as did I. And I did!

Love in a Cardboard Box

One day, many years ago, I asked my mom if she remembered getting a heart-shaped box of candy from my dad every Valentines day. She took me to a closet, and opened the door. Up high on shelves were stacks of empty boxes shaped like a heart with ribbons attached in a variety of colors. She had kept every valentine box she had ever received.

As I looked at them in wonder, I realized that these were not empty boxes, they were boxes full of love. Within these boxes were the memories of receiving each one on the special day for love to be expressed.

Dad always remembered Mom on this day—I saw to it that he remembered. The sight of those boxes proved the effort was well spent, for within was "Love In A Cardboard Box."

There is a lesson to be learned within the experience I just mentioned. A box of candy, a card, whatever the small token may be, you may never realize the significance of the effect and impact it has had. If for only one day out of the entire year, you express your love to someone who cares, that expression of love may be remembered for decades to come.

The heart is known as the place where emotions are born and tend to reside. Sometimes these emotions overshadow our ability to reason. Sometimes our ability to reason overshadow the heart.

It's Not a Smart Thing, It's a Heart Thing

My grandson, Elijah, was the smartest baby on planet Earth when he was just a few months old. I am here to tell you; this kid knew what to do, when to do it, and where and how. We knew then he was going to be a genius just like his papa. One day, however, when my daughter, Donna, walked into the kitchen to fix his bottle, he began crying profusely. She said to me, "Dad, I can't understand how he can be so smart about everything, and not realize that I'm coming back to him as soon as I get his bottle fixed." She was right, I thought. Why would he be acting this way? It was at this point when I received a revelation "on loan from God," as Rush Limbaugh always claims.

It wasn't a smart thing, it was a heart thing. He knew she was coming back. He knew what she was doing. He was just expressing how he missed her presence, her attention, and her devoted love. I said to Donna, "It's not a smart thing, it's a heart thing." As I pondered on the truth of this statement, and how often this is the case in decisions we make, I realized how many things seem foolish, where there is wisdom in the heart, and how many times the heart appears foolish when looked upon by reason.

I could write a book on how many things are done because our "heart voice" tells us to do so, in spite of what the rational mind tells us is the smart thing to do.

Nothing so touches the heart as does an emotional story of someone's life. This became a reality to me when I became acquainted with a young 16-year-old living in the state of California.

Obscure in Oakland

She was weeping, overwhelmed with the sadness from the sense of loss that filled her soul. It was her 16th birthday, a day when most girls are at their fullness of joy. Sixteen! The year you're old enough to drive a car. The beginning of your young adult years. The year, for most, at least, you're surrounded by friends and family, with 16 candles on a special birthday cake.

Not so for Obscure in Oakland. For her it was the day of reckoning, a day of soul searching and taking inventory of her life. It was on this day, this milestone of great significance for a teenager, she had came to the realization that she was not your typical 16-year-old.

If Obscure in Oakland could have made a birthday wish that day, it would have been to be able to erase her past, and begin anew. This would have been the reason for blowing out the 16 candles on the birthday cake she never had that day on her birthday. Listen, attend to her words with your heart, as she describes the story of her life:

"I am 16-years old. I am Filipino French-American. I look Latin or Native American, most say, I was born on Sept. 30, 1979, in Longapo City, Philippines, outside of the former U. S. Sub Bay Naval Station. My father is a French-American (second generation) Navy man; my mom, a university student. My mom gave birth to a child out of wedlock before she had me. The father of my older sister left as soon as he found out my mom was pregnant. After my father and mother were married, we moved to America as citizens of the United States. In 1981 we settled in a navy town, a suburb of San Francisco.

"The day I turned seven, my mom filed for divorce, due to domestic violence, drug and alcohol addictions, Six months later, the divorce became final and my father left the bay area without a trace for two years. At the age of nine my father contacted me and invited me to visit him in Washington, D.C. From the ages of nine to 12, I lived with him in Maryland, Va., area, during which time I was subject to child prostitution and forced into doing a mass quantity and variety of narcotics.

"While living with my father, my mother gave birth to another little girl out of wedlock, giving me a little sister. My mom's childhood was not the kind one learns how to raise a child from as she was physically and mentally abused.

"I have left home for the second time, vowing never to return again. I have lived many places in the past nine months, some stable, some not. At the present, things are much better. I find myself mothering the young people around me. It is a big responsibility. I have many friends, and they say I am as one who has an old soul, where fate has packed double the experience into my 16 years of living.

"I feel my mom has stolen my years of adolescence and killed a part of my life, the part that has diminished. I hate her sometimes, miss her others, but for me, to move home would be suicidal, to my soul and spirit.

"I don't mind sharing my life story and my past, as long as it doesn't come back to haunt me or my friends. Bye, and good night." Obscure in Oakland.

This emotional letter, should be a testimony and a call for prayer for every obscure teenager living this kind of heart breaking life. I have an up side to this story about Obscure in Oakland, I wondered if someone as this, could have any goals or dreams so I asked her. Her response made my heart feel glad and gave me hope for all the youth who have met this fate.

"I am enrolled in a basic education/work experience program of 120 hours. I plan to take the California High School Proficiency Examination and then attend a junior college. I would then like to attend the University of California. I am a writer—non fiction, fiction, playwright, and poetry. I also love music. I play the guitar, piano, and took voice for two years."

In conclusion, "A Heart-To-Heart Message"

When I proudly tell my friends that the thing I love to do most is write articles for my column in TBY, I am often asked, "What do you write about?" or I am asked, "What is a heart article?" After pausing for my thoughts, I tell them I write about things that are on my heart, words that will speak to someone else's heart. It's like a love letter, written heart-to-heart. I have found it is an easy thing to do. But there are guidelines that I adhere to that are a must in writing from the heart.

As much as I love to write humor, I will not write humor in a heart article for sake of writing humor. If it finds its way into a heart article in a sincere honest way I find great joy in writing it. What one finds funny is subject to much opinion. What may be funny to some, may hurt and be painful to others, for one never knows the circumstance the reader may be in at the time it is read.

Sincerity is a must in writing articles from the heart. If I don't mean it, I don't say it! There is a lot of difference in flattery and true praise. I demand from others honesty and truth, and I feel I must give nothing less than what I expect from others. Heart articles must be sincere.

Heart articles must always encourage and be uplifting in a positive manner. Often I will describe a lesson learned, or the results of someone being faced with a set of negative circumstances. I strive to end every article leaving one to think that there is hope and a better way in every situation.

There is too much bad news around already. What one needs, is to hear someone say, "I have good news for you."

When I write a heart article, I may speak about myself, but the article is never written for myself. Every article I write is written for you, the reader. If the article fails to touch you in some way, I have failed to write a heart article. Perhaps it will be the joy of having a grandchild, the pride you have in your community, the sorrow you have experienced in losing a loved one or just things we have shared together, by living here on planet Earth. Every heart article I write is my way of saying I love you, God loves you, and be of good cheer.

I would like to know if "Written From The Heart" has been a joy for you. If it has lifted your heart, brought you a smile or restored your faith in yourself, in man, and in God.

As I sit at night writing articles I hope you are enjoying, I realize you more than likely have some heart stories yourself. I would like to hear from you! I realize you may be more of a reader than a writer since one can hardly get a friend to respond to a letter these days. However, from a friend to a friend, from my heart to yours, I wish to invite you to write whatever is on your heart. After all, this is the month for us "heart people" to share our love with one another.

20

Advice to Son: Car is Like a Woman

My son has a car which we have named Old Blue. Recently, she started acting up while in Jackson as he was on the threshold to take her to Cape. He left her stranded, afraid to push her any more than he already had, as she was acting very much out of her normal disposition.

The next day, as I was taking my son to see her in my car named Big Red, my son began to talk about getting a divorce from Old Blue. He was going to leave her for a truck.

Knowing that he would be making payments on Old Blue even if he went after that truck, I thought it was time for a father-and-son talk about cars being much like women.

"Son," I said, "a car is like a woman. Old Blue has been rather expensive, I will be the first to admit, but she has given you some good times while you have had her. Sure, she needs things once in a while, but they all do, especially when they get a few miles on them. You have to treat them gentle, with tender, loving care. If you give them the needed attention, they will serve you well. Old Blue has sat there all by herself on the side of the road. Who knows, perhaps she will act better now that she has had time to cool off."

I could see the hope in my son's eyes as we approached the area where Old Blue spent the night. It was obvious that he had missed her. Old Blue perked right up when we turned her on, and she purred like a kitten all the way to Cape. As it turned out, she had some water splashed on her, and it upset her ability to perform.

I'm happy to say that my son and Old Blue are lovers again, and that truck has not even been mentioned. Sometimes a father needs to have a father-to-son talk when it comes to women. And cars.

21

Great Physician Relieves All Pain

People are hurting. They are filled with pain that is almost indescribable. Nevertheless, the pain goes unnoticed by others day after day. Pain is an inner feeling, sometimes noticed by a physical expression. Still, pain is as invisible as the air one is breathing.

Pain makes its visitation in two forms: physical and emotional, which are both equal in the effect they have in affecting one's life. Pain cries out seeking to be noticed. However, it is the most misunderstood plea on planet Earth. Almost always, it is cloaked and misconstrued to be something other than pain. This seems to magnify and increase the amount of pain one has.

Pain cannot be seen, but it can be perceived, if one is sensitive to the needs of others. I am very sensitive to pain, both my own and the pain of others. I have found others always relieved and exhilarated to share their pain with me. However, when I try to share my pain with them, I more often than not receive immediate rejection. When this happens, I know whom to call upon who will listen and never reject me. Not only does he welcome my coming to him, he takes away my pain.

How could they have rejected him, and how can one reject him now? If you are hurting, the great physician who specializes in pain is waiting for your call. His name is a name above all names, Jesus Christ.

22

Written in the Wind

Looking at my 1996 calendar, deliberating what I should write for March, I was reminded of what a delightful month March is. There's Saint Patrick's Day! The day I make it a point to wear my color, green.

On the 20th of this month is the first day of spring, my favorite season for sure. On the last day of the month is Palm Sunday, which means Easter is a mere week away. For some reason, my calendar failed to mention two famous birthdays that come in March, my son's, and my grandson's.

So there is much for me to look forward to in March. The symbol that stands out foremost in my mind for the month of March, however, is that March is a windy month. Folks who have mouths that run like a Duracell battery are excused from this flaw, if they happen to be born in the month of March.

Yes, March, is known for producing windy things, so I thought it was only appropriate to write and include some windy tales, about wind, in one fashion or another.

I have three wonderful stories to share that are related to the wind. So lets take a deep breath and begin.

Here with the Wind

On any Thursday or Friday in my home, and within the walls of my wife's beauty shop, you would find a gathering of females, sitting in a circle under hair dryers, reading magazines and looking very innocent and inconspicuous as they partake of this activity on their day's agenda.

They come to get their hair cleaned and styled, hoping to leave looking and feeling more beautiful, this I don't deny. But, men, I wonder if there might be a hidden agenda going on in these beauty salons.

Perhaps a secret conspiracy we have been kept in the dark about, such as a female council, that has shaped and directed our lives for years, with us not even being aware of it.

Have you ever wondered why your wife knew so much about a certain thing you were considering buying or doing? Have you ever wondered how she already had in her hand the decision you were about to make?

As the husband of a hair stylist and shop owner, I have some revealing news for you: There is more in the wind in that beauty shop than hair spray.

Many years ago, I began to notice something was simply not apparent. I would approach the shop full of customers, or the room of "THE COUNCIL OF MAJOR DECISION MAKERS," as you will soon see, and I would hear the sound of laughter and chatter in a non stop fashion. The second my foot hit the beauty shop floor, however, dead silence. All eyes were on me, as if I was a spy from a less than friendly nation.

I let this frequent occurrence pass right on by my highly suspicious nature, with the following justification. I presumed they were talking "women stuff" and since I was a man, they became silent, because women don't talk about their female problems in the presence of a man.

After a few years of complaisance in this troubling observation of sudden silence, I decided to boldly spy on these ladies by placing my ear to the door before walking in on them. The discussion I heard was any and everything but their "latest trip to the doctor." More about this in a moment.

Gentlemen, I fear this thing reaches far beyond my wife's beauty shop. It is bigger than you and me. Consider the number of women attending these meetings, and how many meeting places, or beauty shops, there are. What kind of talk takes place in one of these council meeting you may be asking yourself by now?

CAUTION! Sit down before reading the rest of the story. Are you sitting down?

Every major decision you have ever made was most likely made after you consulted with your wife, right? Surely you at least asked for her input. If for some reason you didn't, I'm sure you received her input anyhow, right?

When she gave you her thoughts about the matter, she astounded you by her knowledge about the decision you were wrestling with. She could tell you story after story of how other people had faced the same situation, what they did about it, and what results they ended up with. She had more information about products than "Good Housekeeping," more knowledge about the practices of business places than the "Better Business Bureau," and more ways to solve emotional family problems than "Dr. Dobson." Whatever it was you planned to do, she had the answer. You couldn't disagree with her, unless you wanted to disagree with a jury of 12 other women who knew she was right!

What man will take on a wife and 12 other women, who know what they are talking about? I've yet to meet such a man. Thus, here is the real reason women get out of their comfortable homes, with their hair looking fearful, and make that trip to the beauty shop. They want to look and feel more beautiful, this I don't deny. But it is that hour spent, sitting with the female council, the hour of power, to assure that women continue to rule the world they really seek.

Women have arrived, and they're "Here With The Wind."

Wind Beneath My Wings

I remember as if it were yesterday, celebrating our 25th wedding anniversary a few years ago. So many friends and relatives came to our reception. And as my wife did her best to let them know how special they were, and how much they meant to us. I looked upon her in awe.

How could I have made it this far in my journey here on earth, without her strength and support. Yes, she was the "Wind Beneath My Wings." There she was, as beautiful as ever, having given birth to three children, and most of her strength in raising them. And while performing this enjoyable task, she worked as a hairdresser. Both of us working together, to make ends meet. Trusting in God always, at least she would. And thank God she did, as I was a worrier.

Whenever life seemed difficult, and I found it hard to rise up to the occasion, she always had the right words to say, which would lift me up and give me courage. She has always had a heart that would rather give than receive. Disagree? At times, but in the end, we would drop selfish pride, because our love for each other was more important than the things we disagreed about.

When a man or a woman faces the storms in life, without some kind of support, they can fall flat on their face. One's spouse can be that support, with God as the foundation.

Whatever I have accomplished in life, certainly did not come without great effort. I can say with much certainty, I am what I am, because my wife is "The Wind Beneath My Wings."

Fishing in the Midst of a Windstorm

Who would think that a windstorm would remain fresh in one's mind, 40 years later in life. I can remember two very clearly.

The first one occurred when I was in the first grade, attending Washington School. I lived in a house where the post office is now located. It was probably the most violent windstorm I can ever remember hitting our city in such a rage. It had been raining very hard, and when the rain slowed down to a sprinkle, the color of the sky became a light shade of green. Suddenly, the wind began shaking the house we were living in. Mom had everyone under a table, except "yours truly," who ran to the window to see what was happening. I couldn't believe what I was seeing. Tables and chairs, trees, and everything but "Mary Poppins" was flying in the air, traveling north passing by our house, like an airborne taxi driving by.

This storm did much damage in the north part of the city, as it passed us by. It seemed to return five years later, beginning right where it had ended the first time around, and just where we happened to be living at the time.

We had added a new member to our family, a dog named "Lady." She never seemed to be afraid of the storms. The wind was furious, and the sky looked a strange color. My mom must have considered this a bad token, as she told everyone, including Lady, to get under a table, and she pushed a cushion chair in front of it, to prevent us from getting cut by broken glass.

My mom, my brother and two sisters, along with me and Lady, got under the table and sat in a very tight circle. I was unaware of the impending danger as was Lady, and wondered why we were sitting under a table. My mom must have been frightened out of her wits, but it never became obvious to us children, who she asked to sing along with her a song. She began to sing, "Follow Me and I'll Make You Fishers of Men." I enjoyed singing and I liked the song, but I thought she was singing "Follow me and I'll Make You A Fisherman."

I wondered why we were singing about going fishing, with such a storm going on outside. The sound of our singing was overpowered by the noise of the wind, which sounded like a train on top of the house. I began to visualize railroad tracks on top of the house, and entertaining thought, when suddenly, Lady, decided to exit our safe harbor, and slipped out between the table and the chair. Seeing that Lady could do it, I decided I would also, and I ran to the window as I had done before, to see what was going on outside.

Finally, I gave in to the pleas of my mom calling me to get back under the table.

When the wind storm had passed over, we went outside to assess the damage. The wind had taken a portion of the roof, and an old shed in the backyard. We were very lucky to be alive. Perhaps it wasn't luck at all. Just maybe, Mom putting her trust in the one who said, "Follow me and I'll make you fishers of men," spared us that day, so we could indeed become followers, and go fishing for lost souls.

23

Don't Let Worries, Fears Take Over

I have spent most of my life failing to live each day to its fullest by letting the worries and fears of tomorrow rob me of the joys of today. For the most part, those worries and fears never took place, hardly ever did they become a reality.

In the past few years, I have learned that, although I don't know what tomorrow holds, I know who holds all of my tomorrows. I guess I have always known this. Nevertheless, I hung onto my right to cling to those worries and fears like they were some kind of priceless possession.

I have sought the answer as to why I would do such a thing. No one seeks these two evils to be his companions for life. My conclusion was it was a matter of trust. I was more willing to live a life full of strife, trusting in myself, that to trust him who brings an end to all strife in one's life.

Why did I find it so difficult to trust God? I suppose part of the reason was because I had learned very early in life that when I trusted people, I got hurt. So often people will let you down. I trusted things. Things will let you down. I trusted religion. Religion will let you down. God had never let me down. Still, I was finding it difficult to trust him.

Why? I think I now know, and if this has been your life, I want to share something very important with you. God will not take anything you are not willing to give. If you want God to take it all, you must be willing to give him all. I wanted God to take my worries and fears, but I was trying to hold on to them at the same time. Trust him. He is faithful and worthy of one's trust.

24

Symphonic Wind Ensemble Delights

What one word would describe the excellent performance presented by the Symphonic Wind Ensemble conducted by Robert M. Gifford last week at Academic Auditorium? The answer is serendipity. I was expecting an evening of wonderful music performed by students with exceptional musical ability under the direction of a professional conductor. I received all that I was expecting and much more.

During the final composition, "The Stars and Stripes Forever," the audience was invited to participate with the wind ensemble by clapping hands with the cadence of this most loved march.

Serendipity: finding something better than what you were looking for.

25

My Little Corner of the World

For the past 20 years, I have been living within a rocks throw of the neighborhood where I grew up as a child. Standing on my back porch, looking at the small, but priceless earthly soil I call my backyard, I can recall playing with friends on this very spot. Some things have changed within these four city blocks of which I live, and where I lived as a child but many things have remained the same.

I am constantly reminded of the events that occurred during this time of my life. A time and place where there is a thousand stories to be told. Come along with me. "To My Little Corner Of The World."

"The Alley"

Each day I observe the alley that has stood the test of time and remains from the days of my youth. This alley was part of my financial empire when I was a boy. From this alley I reaped the wealth it contained by walking through it daily, collecting copper wire that brought me 10 cents a pound. The hard part was cleaning it before taking it to the salvage yard, which meant burning the outer coating off, the cloth or rubber part. I also collected soda bottles, which were returnable for cash.

Then there was the old shed that sat in our backyard by the alley. I earned 50 cents a week there, keeping a close eye on the car a businessman owned and wanted to park there, to keep it out of the bad weather.

It was this very alley that a daily traveler walked. His lifestyle has remained firmly in my mind. Today, he would be called an alcoholic or a wine-o. I reckon that is what grownups called him back then, too. I would see him daily in this alley, looking in the trash cans for any bottle that had alcohol listed as its contents. And he promptly drank those contents, to the bottom of the bottle, if there was any left to be consumed.

I never learned his real name, but I watched for him to come down the alley, searching for those bottles of his choice. He was not a social type of a fellow, never said a word with the exception of one. His tall frail body was a reflection of his liquid diet I suppose. Once, when I got close enough to see them, I noticed how his despondent eyes sank deep into his head. He looked very frail and feeble, and would scare many, if not most, kids who crossed his path. I never feared him, however, as I felt he was trespassing in my alley. I did keep a close eye on him while he paid little attention to me.

One would have thought he was unaware I was anywhere near him. He never picked up anything worthwhile in my alley. He even left the copper that brought 10 cents a pound! I didn't mind him going through the trash, as long as he left my spending money things behind. He never took a single soda bottle, the only bottles he wanted were perhaps hair tonic, or mouthwash bottles which contained his much needed ingredient.

I never questioned how or why he became the person that he was. Nevertheless, I will never forget this old man, who never hurt anyone to my knowledge, other than himself by drinking so much. Though we never knew each others name, we had a form of communication we shared each and every time we saw each other.

I would shout out the word "watermelon" and with a weakness in his voice, he would reply with the word "cantaloupe."

"The Birthday"

Standing in my backyard, looking south toward the yard I played in as a child, there is a black top parking lot in between. This parking lot was there when I was a child, and it brings back memories of a birthday party which took place on this very lot.

The birthday boy was Jerry, and it was at this birthday party I learned how difficult it is to whistle after eating a mouthful of crackers. Thinking of Jerry's birthday reminds me of a very special birthday I had about that same time period.

My birthday comes in January, right after Christmas. Today, it seems, Christmas comes for children once a day all year long. When I was a child, buying toys for one's children for Christmas was a year round project, meaning parents paid for those toys for the next 12 months. So, I never expected much for my birthday.

Mom always made me a birthday cake, and served it on a beautiful green platter, a gift she received at a birthday party on her birthday in 1935, eight years before I was born. That cake was served with love, and if that was all there was, I would have been happy. I never had a wagon or a tricycle. I didn't miss them that much to tell you the truth. I was quite content with my metal toy cars and trucks.

My favorite toys were actually a June bug tied to a string, to play with during the day, and a jar full of lightning bugs or fire flies some folks call them, to play with at night.

This year was different however, as I had seen a bright red shiny scooter that I simply fell in love with. I knew Mom and Dad could not afford this scooter, and I never expected them to get it for me. I was so in love with this two-wheel thing I simply could not stop talking about it. When I went to bed the night before my birthday, I fell asleep expecting to receive perhaps two shiny quarters for my birthday, which would be equal to two weeks allowance.

When I awoke, I thought I was having a dream. I said to myself, "I must be dreaming, I see a bright red scooter sitting beside my bed." I reached out my hand to touch it, expecting it to go away. After feeling the smooth metal and the rubber handles, suddenly I knew it wasn't a dream. It was a scooter for me, given by two parents who loved me very much, and who were willing to sacrifice to see that I had it. It was the greatest birthday I ever had!

As my eyes return to the alley, which leads to Good Hope Street, the memories of a red shoeshine kit, still lingers in my mind.

Shoe Shine Boy

I was only eight years old, and I had just attended a summer vacation Bible school for the first time. After a week of lessons and fellowship, I left the large Methodist church with a bright red, wooden shoeshine kit. It was the craft I had chose to make while I was there. I admired how well it was made, but I wondered why I had chose to make it. I had never shined my shoes before and certainly no one else's. "But why not?" I thought. If Mom would loan me a dollar, I could be in business for myself. I would buy a can of black and a can of brown shoe polish, find a nice clean cloth and a brush, and hit the streets.

So this is what I did. Good Hope Street, was a busy section of town, two blocks from where I lived. Up and down this street I went with my shoeshine kit. Offering to shine people's shoes for a "dime a shine." And I did well.

I made around $2 on weekdays, and as much as $5 on Saturdays. Most folks gave me two dimes or a quarter, instead of the dime I was charging. Not bad for an 8-year old in 1951!

It was summer and the weather was hot. After a week or so, I noticed everyone staying inside, trying to stay cool. The beer taverns on Good Hope and Sprigg Street were full of people. I was determined not to be out done by the sun and I said to myself, "If you want customers, you must go where they are at."

Having said this, I boldly walked through the door of the Sprigg Street Tavern, which was just around the corner of Good Hope Street. The owner and bartender, whose name was Henry, immediately came up to me as I entered. I was afraid he was going to ask me to leave. With a most serious look on his face, Henry asked, "Do you have a union button?" I was taken completely by surprise, as I had never heard of a union, certainly not a shoeshine union. With a quiver in my voice, I looked up at the tall, slim owner and said, "No sir, I don't." Having said this, Henry walked over to the cash register, and returned with a blue, bartender union button. "Here!" he said. "If you want to work in my place, you must have a union button. When you go to the other taverns, tell them Henry gave you this union button, and said it was okay for you to come in."

I did well that day and the days that followed, thanks to my friend Henry. Not only at the Sprigg Street Tavern, but the other taverns as well. For I was welcomed everywhere with my red shoe shine kit and my blue shoeshine button!

Conclusion

We are observing a strange paradox taking place in our cities and towns. As the population increases and people live closer to each other, relationships and communication between neighbors are drifting further apart. It is not unusual in apartment complexes, to have people living a wall space away from each other, and still not know each others names. Not uncommon are homes a few feet away from each other, where a decade can pass and the owners of these homes are not able to tell you who lives next door. Even relatives, who live a few city blocks from each other, may only visit each other once a year, if then. The historic magic of neighbors and relatives caring for each other, or just dropping by to say hello, is swiftly becoming the lost dinosaur. The kind of magic that existed in, "My Little Corner Of The World."

26

In the End, Truth is Still Truth

You can twist me, bend me, cover me and color me. You can change the meaning of every word in the dictionary and use them in the cleverest fashion. You can change the tone of your voice and your facial expression, and you can point your finger in someone's face. You can create distractions which cover the entire globe. You can enlist the most excellent of legal experts and men who have sworn to honor me and have them try to discredit me. In the end, you will be required to face and accept me. I am the truth.

27

Young Band's Fans Barred

They never had a chance going in, as they took the stage at the River City Yacht Club that evening of March 21. This fact, however, could not be observed by an unknowing observer in the crowd. The three teenagers took their musical instruments up in arms and gave a brilliant performance, a performance that held the attention of fans of the competing band. The event was the semifinals of the Q99 Battle of the Bands.

With only a few months to practice to become a band, never having performed before a crowd or any audience other than their fans who came to hear them practice, these three 17-year-old young men had found their way to the semifinals among bands who had performed often for a large following of fans and who were devoted in supporting them. These three teenagers also had developed a large following, but they were not allowed in because of their age. These fans were the same fans who voted for them repeatedly by calling Q99 and the station welcomed their calls. Now their votes were denied at a time when their votes would really count.

For the benefit of the many fans who were not allowed to see and hear "Sinclair" perform, I am pleased to inform that you would have been proud. As a father of one of the band members, I want to thank you for your support. I would also encourage radio stations that decide to have a band contest in the future to either put an age limit on those entering the contest or have the finals where no age limit is enforced.

28

Little Paws Keep Stepping on My Heart

The kind of animals you have for pets, such as cats and dogs, you either love them or you don't. I always have, and my wife never has—loved them, that is. My mom recently told me how, when I began walking to school in the first grade, this little dog mysteriously appeared to walk me there. Mom went on to say he was always waiting for me to walk me home, too. We never knew where he came from or where he went. Nevertheless, having him with me made me feel safe in the long walk to school I made each day.

Twelve years ago, after losing my French poodle, which was hit by a car, my children thought I would feel better if I went to get another poodle. So to please the kids, in spite of my wife's firm rebuttal that it was a huge mistake, we went to get one. They only had one left, a male, black with a white streak running down his back and tummy. I paid the $100 and my wife agreed to hold him on her lap as we drove home. I asked the kids what we should name him, and before they had a chance to make a suggestion, my wife said we should name him Skunk or Skunky since he looked like a skunk.

We all agreed, amazed that the only member of our family who hated animals was not only holding this dog on her lap, but wanted to be the one to name it.

A few years later, we inherited a cat from our daughter. Her name is Katy, and we call her Katy Bear. She and Skunk have become quite a pair, and I would like to share a few tales about these two who keep walking on my heart.

Oh What a 'Birdie-Full' Morning

I was awakened one morning with a bright light blinding me and my wife flapping her arms up and down. "Why does it sound like a bird flapping its wings?" I thought. Then, the sound of her thunderous voice said, "There's a bird in our furnace, and it's trying to get out. If it gets out, it will knock over and break everything."

Sure enough, the small closet area, where our gas furnace is located to provide heat for our bedroom, had a bird trapped behind its folding access doors. I was more concerned about the bird than my wife's pretty breakables. "We need to get it out. If we don't, it will get hurt," I pleaded. This plea didn't seem to put a caring expression on my wife's face so I tried another one.

"If Katy Bear gets it, she will kill it." I no more than got the words "Katy Bear" out of my mouth, when who do you think was waiting in front of the folding doors. None other than Katy, the midnight stalker. I thought the bird would come out flying, and since Katy had not learned to fly, as yet, the bird would be safe. Wrong! The second I opened the doors, the bird came out at a low level, and Katy, bird in mouth, took off running faster than a Kentucky Derby winner, "Man Of War." As for myself, who had not had his first cup of coffee, I took off after them several laps behind. I trapped Katy at the top of a flight of stairs, and insisted she release the bird. She slowly let it fall from her mouth, which was still full of feathers, and to my amazement the bird flew away, back to my bedroom. So I returned to where this adventure had begun. I kept lunging for the bird, falling way short of Katy's ability to reach it. When I finally got the bird out of the bedroom, Katy was waiting for it in the adjoining room, and with bird in mouth once again, she took off into the living room.

My wife had informed me that Katy was in the living room, but there was no bird in her mouth. Looking at Katy, who was all stretched out laying on the floor, I asked, "What happened to the bird?" as if she was going to answer me. Katy gave me a look of complete contentment and I knew. Yes, I knew, she must have eaten that little bird. Swallowed it in one bite! At least it's over, I thought. Then, Katy arose from the floor and from beneath her, came that little bird, still able to fly, like a swift moving space shuttle. It was off to the races again. Only this time, I was saying, "Katy, get that bird, catch it." I was getting tired of this silly game. I knew Katy had the ability to find the bird, and would be able to catch it. Why should I be left alone to do all the work? I opened both doors that go outside so the bird could leave, but instead, the bird performed flybys and landed everywhere else.

I thought the comment my wife had made about knocking things over and breaking them was silly, until the bird landed on my $200 scanner radio. I screamed, "Katy get this bird, eat the thing!" By now, I had no respect for the bird's intelligence, and very little love for it as one of God's creatures, at least for that moment. Afraid that I might do more damage to the house than the cat or bird would, my wife and son came to help me with the problem. The three of us were able to guide the bird out an opened door and all was well. Oh, what a birdie-full morning.

Tea Time

Just when I am four payments away from having my house paid for, I find I am but a tenant. The real owners and rulers of my house are Katy and Skunky. What a rude awakening, but it's true. Permit me to explain.

When I first arise in the morning, getting out of bed carefully so that I don't disturb Katy, who is sleeping on my feet. Skunky is waiting for me to open the door for him so he can go outside. This, mind you, is not a request, it is a demand. If I don't let him outside, he has proven what the consequences will be, and his "Wetting" is worse than his wiggle when insisting he wants outside. Thus, before my first cup of coffee, I become his servant. While my coffee is perking, so am I, filling his food and water dish. The smell of the food gets Katy up and, somehow, she communicates to Skunky how I forgot to give them treats last night and they both stand at the refrigerator and make strange noises until I pop open the container that holds the expensive "canned delight" they both love.

This gives me the chance to get ready for work and make my great escape from this house of slavery. Having a few moments to watch the news on TV before leaving, I decided to sit down in what used to be my comfortable chair. With Katy and Skunky sleeping on it, I feel obligated to kindly ask them to get off. They look at me like they have just won the lottery and go back to sleep. Giving up, I step out into their beautiful back yard, full of green grass and play my version of hop scotch, trying to make it to the car without stepping on what Skunky has been using to make it so green.

After working all day to pay the house payment and the utility bill, I come home to hungry creatures of God, who allow me to fix them their dinner, change the litter box, and sit by their side, while I am trying to have dinner myself. They insist, however, that I give them at least a 10th of what I eat, in little bites thrown on the new carpet they love to do their exercises on.

On a good day, I get to read the paper before Katy decides she wants to lie on it, or read a book for two whole minutes without getting up out of my chair to come to their every whim or whine. Don't get me wrong, it's not like they never do their part, as owners of what used to be my home.

Katy stays up almost all night, prowling the house, searching for anything that crawls in the dark. I know this to be true as she will knock over and break anything to stop them from their madness. This brings Skunky into action with his "somebody is in the house" barking, and things don't settle down until I get up to investigate. After doing so, they will give me that you did well look, and I can go back to bed and try to get some sleep. Sleep is something I'm in much need of, if I am to get up the next day, to pay the price of living in a house that I once thought was mine.

As for now, however, I must run, as I have got to fix tea for two.

29

Don't Stop Liberty Bell's Ringing

Will the Liberty Bell cease to let freedom ring? In the Untied States—where democracy has been more than just a theory, where freedom has played such an important role in shaping the world around us—before our very eyes we are watching our freedom being taken away. It began when we started taking freedom for granted in the midst of aggressive forces determined to have other forms of government prevail. This was followed by apathy. We surrendered our minds to the demands of those whom we placed in office. What would Thomas Jefferson say of this generation? He said, "I have sworn upon the altar of God eternal hostility against every form of tyranny over the mind of man."

We are living in a democracy, and freedom is the essence of democracy. But we have surrendered such freedoms as our right to speak our minds openly to praise or criticize the government, support the part in power or organize opposition parties. It appears we are a far cry from a dictatorship. However, the frog in the water which was slowly warming would never have believed that it would ever reach a temperature which would cause his existence to cease.

Some argue that the United States is not a democracy and was never meant to be. There is the view that our Founding Fathers intended the nation to take the form of a republic. In 1787, the word "democracy" meant something other than what it means today. Most of the Founding Fathers intended the new government to be based on the consent of the people. It would be impossible for all citizens to make the laws and carry them out.

But with every new law intended to make our world a better place to live, there comes the price of freedom. Benjamin Franklin said, "They that give up essential liberty to obtain a little temporary safety deserve neither liberty or safety."

So, on what road do we travel? Are we heading toward the path of a new revolution? Or shall we some morning wake up to a form of government our country once despised?

In the eyes of the world, the Berlin Wall once stood as a symbol of rule by tyranny, just as the Liberty Bell today symbolizes freedom. John F. Kennedy said, "The cost of freedom is always high, but Americans have always paid it." Are we willing to pay the price? If we are, we will let our voices be heard throughout the world, demanding a voice in the important decisions that affect our lives. If this should fail to happen, the Liberty Bell will cease to let freedom ring.

30

Drawing the Line on Exploration

When my grandson, Elijah, lived in Dallas, he so desperately wanted a pet he would immediately claim and give a name to every insect that crossed his path. On one of my visits, Elijah had detected an ant living outside on the porch in front of the apartment door. When he saw it, he exclaimed, "Look, Papa, there's"—at which point he called out a name I could not pronounce or even begin trying to spell. He knelt down and began speaking to that ant like it was his best friend.

He had to be at school in a matter of minutes and asked me if I would stay with his little friend. I told him of course I would be glad to, thinking the moment he was out of sight I would be able to go back inside and perhaps get another hour's sleep. I watched that little ant with Elijah until he had to leave, and in doing so I was fascinated by how busy that ant was in the small world he was living in.

Most likely, that ant never went any farther in his entire life than that porch. I pondered how what he knew was all within the small confines of his limited personal world. As I continued my train of thought, it occurred to me that this minute world he lived in was an extremely small portion of a much larger world. Such as the one my cat Katy Bear lives in.

The ant would have had a very short life if he had lived within the confines of Katy Bear's world. She loves killing bugs and performs this feat better than people I have paid to eliminate these pests. Katy is a house cat, and with the exception of a few breakouts into the back yard, the house she lives in is her world. All that she knows is within the small confines of her personal limited world, my house, which is but a small portion of a much larger world.

In bringing this full circle, I thought of us humans. What we know is within the small confines of the limited world we live in, a world which could contain enduring facts and truths of a much larger world. If the ant decided he wanted to discover and live in the world my cat lives in, he would find that survival in her world would be impossible. Since my cat has lived her total existence in the confines of my house, she would find survival in my world short-lived at the very most. She would also discover she was living in a world of inventions and lifestyles she was not designed for or capable of ever utilizing.

Thus, what does mankind hope to achieve? What benefit will there be in finding a larger world? It would be a world of inventions and lifestyles in which we could not exist. Man has always been driven by a magnificent desire to discover what is there which we do not know. This leaves me to believe that the creator of our world has drawn a line which we cannot cross or perhaps had better not cross. Heaven help us if it is the latter of the two.

31

School: A Sentimental Journey

When I was in the third grade at Lorimier Elementary, I would walk to school each day. Walking to school wasn't much fun, because I had to be there right on time. This left no time for me to explore the surroundings that fascinated me so.

Walking home, however, was a different story. My mom either didn't have a clock or was not sure when school let out because I never arrived at home as soon as school was over. Every day my walk home was an adventure. One of my walking home activities was stopping at a house, walking up to their front porch and knocking on the door. When someone came to the door, I would inform them that I was a car salesman.

Almost everyone I approached ordered a car and some even bought two! I would ask them what color they would like their car to be and then pretend to write it down.

And with a limited number of houses to call on, I had many repeat customers. This basic training in "COLD CANVAS SELLING" as it is called, became a valuable asset 20 years later, when I was selling life insurance door to door.

When not selling cars, I was searching for the homeless—animals, that is. I have always loved animals, especially dogs and cats. I tried to convince every animal I would see when walking home that they should follow me and let me take good care of them for the rest of their lives. A few took me up on my offer and, fortunately for me, my mom and dad loved pets as well. Whether I was selling cars or bringing home creatures, walking home was a joy, even when I walked in the snow and rain.

One day, in the month of December, it had snowed and my mom let me wear my galoshes to school. By the end of the school day the snow had melted, so I, of course, left my galoshes at school. My mom kept insisting, as moms always do, that I should bring them home. So one beautiful day in the first part of June I thought I might surprise her and do just that!

When the school day was over, I put those galoshes over my shoes and headed for home. Everyone driving by me in their cars were slowing down, smiling and waving. I smiled too, thinking that they were enjoying seeing a child in oversized galoshes on a bright sunny day. Not once had the thought of carrying them home ever occurred to me for I knew I would need my two hands for the place where I was going before going home.

To Begin at Happy Hollow

The most exciting way to walk home was to begin at Happy Hollow, a mystic land of wilderness, just south of the school.

Happy Hollow was an experience that could be termed a child's "imaginary heaven." There was quicksand there and if you fell in you would never be seen again. At least that's the story we would tell those afraid to go there. I did see a shoe and a stick get swallowed up in that sink hole once and to the best of my knowledge they never came back.

One could also swing on giant grapevines as Tarzan did, over a river. (Actually it was a small stream.) Several of us third-graders enjoyed playing in this scenic place. After playing for perhaps an hour or so, we would walk up the railroad tracks and set a penny on the narrow metal rail, in hopes it would be made the size of a quarter by the oncoming train.

They always fell off before the train arrived for some reason. This disappointed me because I really wanted to see one of those pennies after a train ran over it.

Happy School Hour

Lest I have you thinking I hated school, not all of my happy memories are after school memories. There were some good times to be had during the school day.

Take play day, for instance. I always looked forward to play day. There were potato sack races and the three-legged race, of which I always brought home ribbons, making my mom so proud.

Then there were the school plays. I was always the star attraction in the school plays. I was very small for a child in the third grade. In fact, I looked like a first-grader. Looking like a first-grader in a third-grade play was cute, I must admit. It made me look like a child prodigy and the audience loved it. I was always trying to be funny and always showing off. I remember once teaching the girls in a production of, "The Easter Parade," how they should walk across the stage.

I must have done well, as they continued to walk that way in their teens.

I loved performing. Once I was the star in a musical, along with a girl named Jane, and we did an Irish dance. Jane had a twin brother Jerry and we became friends. I still see Jerry today from time to time and visit with Jane and Jerry's mom, whom I never had met as a child.

Jane was a good friend but the girl I fell in love with was named Bonnie. I made my mom tired of a song, one she once enjoyed. I sang "My Bonnie Lies Over The Ocean," night after night all night long. I loved Bonnie until I made it to junior high, along with 10 or 20 others I met along the way. Yes, I was a typical child in the third grade, wasn't I? I had goals, and ambitions, dreams and hopes. I knew what I wanted on any given day which was never the same as the day before.

Left Ain't Right, But It Ain't Wrong

My third grade teacher did not like me, and I have been searching for a reason since I first sat in her class room. I remember several things she did not like, things I did that upset her. However, I feel the thing that troubled her most was that I was left-handed. This was not well accepted by teachers in those days and it frustrated her when I would not be persuaded to use my right hand, or failed to be able to use it with accuracy. As punishment she kept me after school and had me hold out my left hand as she struck it with a ruler until it was sore. I suppose she thought if my left hand became disabled I would begin to use my right.

One day she announced to the class that a national safety organization was having a contest and we were to write an essay on safety. I was almost too afraid to write anything, considering how she felt about me writing left handed. As the other students got out their pencils and paper, proceeding to write several pages, I just sat holding a pencil thinking about how I was worried about my dad drinking and driving a car.

Suddenly, I noticed I was the only student in the room and my teacher was standing at my desk. She said, "Are you done with your essay?" I told her I had thought of nothing to write. She looked at me with fury and shouted "Think, think, think!" I took my pencil in my left hand and wrote three words on the piece of paper, "Think, don't drink." After I handed it to her, I never thought about it again until 20 years later.

When I was driving on the highway, I saw a large sign that said, yep, you guessed it, "Think, don't drink." It was an ad for the National Safety Council. Do you suppose?

Did I miss school? Sometimes yes, sometimes no. I am convinced that schools have improved dramatically in the past few decades. This certainly includes teachers. Every teacher I know is a beautiful person. On the other hand, my right one of course, I realize they're not my teachers, they're my friends. It's the long walk home that I miss.

Strangely, I walk an identical path each day going to work as the one I walked going to school. I even walk to Happy Hollow and the old railroad tracks. As it was back then, walking home is a different story. Nevertheless, it's just a continuation of life's journey that began with that first step to school.

32

When All is Said and Done...

When love is my response to anger,
When kindness is my reward for hate,
When mercy is my antidote for justice,
When patience means far more than wait,
When God's word is heard when I speak,
When I give all my strength unto the weak,
When I'm on my knees more than my feet,
When I see God in those I meet,
When my flesh becomes my slave,
When I feel peace unto the grave,
When the friends who I bring home
Are poor and all alone,
When I deny my selfish pride
To save hurt feelings they can't hide,
When I am true to his word employ,
When all of life is full of joy,
Then I will be
God's precious fruit.

33

We Can Help the Loneliest People

I was once asked the question in a self-evaluation test, "If you could meet any living person in the world, who would it be?" I gave this question more consideration than all the other questions on the test. I wanted to be absolutely honest with myself in answering.

As I searched my heart for the most honest answer I could give, the question became a challenge. Would it be the president of the United States? Would it be a king or queen, or perhaps the pope or Billy Graham?

After a long deliberation, I took my pen and wrote the answer. If I could meet any living person in the world, I would want to meet the loneliest person in the world.

What a sad title it would be for a person to hold: the loneliest person in the world. Can anyone imagine how that person would feel if they could actually lay hold to such a claim?

Millions of human beings have thought at some point and time in their life that they were qualified to make such a claim. I would not exclude myself from this march to Lonely Street.

There was once a song titled "Lonely Street." It was about a place where broken hearts meet.

I have said all of the above to inform you who feel lonely, who feel qualified to be the loneliest person in the world, that there is such a place as Lonely Street. The good news is that God takes up residence there, waiting and wanting to fellowship and to heal your broken heart. That is why I wanted to meet the loneliest person in the world: to inform him he need not be lonely anymore. God's love will fill that empty spot in his soul and mend that broken heart.

34

Summertime Vacations and the Joys of Indian Creek

My father's parents had a farm in Indian Creek. Many of my summers were spent visiting them for a week. When not spending a week with my grandparents during the summer, I would try to visit an aunt and uncle who lived in the country. It was there I discovered that the grandest place for a city boy to get away from it all, is in "Country Land."

"Country Land…A Dream Vacation"

Permit me to take you on a trip, not to Disney World, not to Disneyland. A summer vacation in every child's vacation spot that should be in every child's dream, "Country Land." As a child, I was fortunate enough to make this trip almost every summer, for one whole week! Where is "Country Land?" If your grandparents lived in the country, and you were a city boy, you had one to visit.

For me, it began by crawling in the back of my uncle's pickup truck, and bouncing along as he drove down the blacktop road, to the gravel road, to grandma's house. This ride, in itself, was worth more than all the money I've spent on rides at amusement parks; turning and twisting at fast speeds down the bumpy road; the scenery constantly changing, from the business of the city to the serene atmosphere of the country.

When we arrived at the welcome center, "Grandma's house," she would always be happy to see me. Why, you would have thought that I was a paying guest. She would help me take the clothes I had packed, to the penthouse (actually, the attic) and then she would show me the large bed I would get to sleep in, all by myself. This in itself, was very special, as at home I would have to share a bed with my brother. Then, she would offer me something to eat.

I was always too excited to eat, because I couldn't wait to see the exotic animals. There were horses, cows, pigs, even a bull. My favorite of all her animals were two dogs named "Bossy and Bouncer." They were very large dogs, with deep voices, and wide backs on which I could ride.

One afternoon, I decided to take a walk in the woods behind my grandparent's house, and I took Bouncer with me. After an hour or so, I walked into a clearing in the middle of the woods, completely surrounded by brush and trees. In the center of this clearing, was what appeared to be Indian graves. Three eight foot diameter circles, with the most beautiful rocks and stones around the circles to mark them off. I was so fascinated by this find in the woods, I had lost track of time. I noticed the sun was going down, and it was beginning to get dark in the midst of the tall trees surrounding me. As I looked to see which way I had come into the clearing, I discovered that in every direction the view was the same. I was lost, and scared! I had forgotten about Bouncer, when suddenly, I heard him begin to bark with that low sounding bark he could make. He was standing at the edge of the clearing, with his head motioning toward the trees. Thinking of what Lassie would say if she was doing that, I realized Bouncer was saying, "Come on, I know how to get us back!" I shouted, "Go home Bouncer—go home." Bouncer began running through the trees as I kept shouting, "Go home Bouncer, go home." Bouncer did go home, and I had someone to follow that day. Someone who took me out of the coming darkness, and calmed my fears of being lost. Feeling lost is a terrible feeling.

Before evening would fall, Grandma would do the craziest thing I had ever seen. She was quite a performer! She would run after her chickens until she caught one, grab it by the neck, and whip it around in a circle until its head came off. This would have me laughing right up till dinner time. I wonder why we always had fried chicken for dinner? Whatever the reason, it sure was good.

They go to bed early at "Country Land." This doesn't mean you have to go to sleep, however, I would sit by the window and feel the cool summer breeze while smelling the hay. Hearing the sounds of the crickets relaxed me so much, I would soon be rubbing my eyes and pulling the sheet over my very tired body.

With the rising of the sun, the rooster would crow, and Grandma would be in the kitchen, making me chocolate gravy and eggs and biscuits. A better breakfast cannot be found. Then out the door I would run, to climb up on Grandpa's tractor, sit in the hot metal seat, and pretend I was king of the road. Then, barefoot, I would hop down the old gravel road to the little country store, a half-mile from Grandma's house, and buy a chocolate soda pop. Close by was the creek, where the fish jumped high out of the water, I would sometimes find an arrowhead rock or perhaps, one, that almost was.

By late afternoon, when my uncles and aunts had finished their work, they would come over to Grandma's house, and entertain me with their fiddles and guitars—making music suitable for Opryland. But I was not at Opryland, nor was I at Disneyland, I was at the greatest vacation spot in the whole wide world! I was at "Country Land."

The Country Boy Dare Devil

My Aunt Maxine and Uncle Omar lived less than a half mile down the rock-covered road from Grandma's house. I spent much of my time visiting with them during the day, as my cousins who were about my age lived there. We would get to play games together, when they were not working on the farm, which they did very often. One day I was playing all alone at my Aunt Maxine's, riding a tricycle that belonged to one of my cousins. My legs were very strong as a child, and I had that three-wheel machine traveling fast through the thick grass in her front yard. Suddenly, I spotted the large dump hole in the front yard, which we had been warned about repeatedly to stay away from. It was a deep hole filled with broken glass and opened tin cans. It appeared to be around six feet across. I began thinking about what an accomplishment it would be to get that tricycle running really fast, and just fly right over that big old hole, plumb to the other side, without ever touching the ground. I was convinced I could do it! So off I went as fast as I could pedal, but when I came to that hole, I didn't go air borne as I thought I would. Instead, I did a flip and landed on my head, which landed on an open tin can. I received a horrible cut. By the time I crawled out of that hole and made it to my aunt's front door, blood was rushing down my face. I must have looked something fearful, because my aunt began crying and screaming. She picked me up and put me in her car, and with the gas pedal to the floor, Aunt Maxine got me to Grandma's house in less than a minute. At least it seemed that way. After several people, along with Grandma, looked at my wound while keeping an ice pack on it, they decided I wouldn't need stitches. I suppose Aunt Maxine still remembers that occurrence, when I decided I was the "Country Boy Dare Devil."

A Place Where Love and Blackberries Grow

More than one summer of my childhood was spent at my Aunt Margie's and Uncle Joe's farm. It was located directly across from Trail of Tears Park. I reckon back then, part of their farm, was Trail of Tears Park. Aunt Margie treated me as one of her own. She had three children, all living at home at the time, but she always had room for one more, such as I, when I would ask to come and visit. I remember Aunt Margie and Uncle Joe as soft spoken people, who displayed a tremendous amount of patience and love. Love was felt in that house, always!

They went to bed early at Aunt Margie's house, but would be up with the sun to milk the cows. I tagged along a few times to observe this chore. I might have tried it once or twice, I can't recall for sure. I do remember two horses on the farm, as I would go horseback riding with my cousin, Kay. My horse would follow commands, not my commands, however. Whatever Kay commanded her horse to do, my horse would do likewise. This was scary for me, as Kay was an experienced rider, and I would only get to sit upon a horse once a year.

My most favorite remembrance of vacationing at Aunt Margie's was the blackberries. Oh, how I loved her blackberry cobbler! I remember hanging around the kitchen, asking my Aunt Margie a thousand questions, knowing she would run out of answers, then hand me a large one gallon pail and say, "Here, go fill this up with blackberries, and I will fix you blackberry cobbler tonight." Yes, the place that set my heart aglow, was a place where love and blackberries grow.

Even today, I find something calling my heart back to these familiar places. Once in awhile, on a Sunday afternoon, I take a drive out highway 177, past Trail Of Tears park and pass my Aunt Margie's farm. I then continue driving, until I can swing around and head back to town, by coming through Indian Creek, past my Grandmother's farm. Seeking to feel once again, the joy that was mine, during my summer vacations and visits to Indian Creek.

35

Important World News Squeezed Out

As I write this letter, the allegations linking Monica Lewinsky to President Clinton continue to increase by the second. It has dominated and commanded news coverage to such an extreme that much of the other news is not being reported.

Consider what brought this to my attention. While listening to the radio on Jan. 23, I thought I heard someone say, "The State Department has issued a warning that it is not safe to travel to Bosnia or Croatia." Having a daughter and grandson living in Croatia, this news was of much concern. The person reporting this statement did not explain why it was unsafe as he quickly and casually tossed in this news item somewhere between Kenneth Starr and President Clinton's problems.

I listened for more news about the State Department's statement the rest of the day to no avail. When I spoke to my daughter in Croatia the next day, she quickly informed me that the American embassy in Croatia had called her two days ago and advised her to be cautious. The reason for the call was a situation that took place in that part of the country that might cause retaliation against Americans living there, an event that at any other time would have been in the news.

When I asked my daughter if she had heard about what was happening in the news we have been receiving about this scandal, she informed me she had not heard anything at all about it. She was very surprised by the news and went on to say that President Clinton's popularity was very high with the people who live in Croatia.

By no means do I wish to lessen the importance of the possibility that the president may be forced to resign or be impeached. Nevertheless, one must wonder what thoughts are in the minds of parents who have children in the Gulf area where we may soon be at war. What would they want to hear on the news: a thousand allegations or what their children may be facing in a matter of a few weeks?

36

Where is Proof of the Allegations?

I read in disbelief the reported comments and allegations state Sen. Peter Kinder was quoted as saying in the front-page article, "Group of lawmakers pushes impeachment," Nov. 7. In this article, Kinder said, "I believe Bill Clinton is an appallingly corrupt president, the most corrupt we have ever had. I believe he and his wife have probably been involved in obstruction of justice, corrupting the FBI, the IRS and other abuses. Janet Reno is a joke at the Justice Department, the FBI has been compromised." There was more, but I believe this is sufficient enough to make my point.

These are some serious allegations. My disbelief was not founded on the fact that these allegations might be true. I was thunderstruck that an individual who has been entrusted to an office such as Kinder has been would so casually make such statements unless he was willing and able to prove them.

I have a great amount of respect for all that Kinder fights for and the beliefs he stands for in keeping and reestablishing moral values in our land. Nevertheless, it is my firm conviction that when a person who holds such an office as Kinder does, one should exercise extreme discipline in judgment and use wisdom in speaking of those who hold such positions as Janet Reno and Bill Clinton. Any dog can bark in his own back yard. It is the dog who considers his foe and his intentions before sounding the warning who receives the most respect from both its owner and any intruder.

Once Kinder called me into his office at the Missourian and politely informed me that the newspaper could not publish a poem I had written about an earth-quake. The reason it could not be published, according to Kinder, was because I could not prove the area was going to have an earthquake. It was an allegation and not a fact. Does Kinder think that it is all right for him to make allegations about the president of the Untied States without proof and wrong for me to write a poem about an alleged earthquake because it might instill fear in the hearts of newspaper's readers? My mom used to always say something I never understood until now: What's good for the goose is good for the gander. Somehow it seems to fit here.

Lest I be misunderstood, this letter is not in defense of the man holding the office of president. When he was reelected, my own personal thought was that God must be using him to punish our nation for the sins it had committed. For whatever reason he was reelected. He holds the highest office in our land. And that office is still to be respected, as should the person who holds that office still be respected until there is absolute proof he is unfit for that office.

37

Things that I Find Strange

We are living in day and age where the term "strange," has become the norm. Our minds have been so conditioned to things that once seemed unusual, that now, it is hard to really point out something we can call strange. A typical conversation, that might be heard today, would be as such, "Don't you find it strange that her hair is purple?" "No, not really, it goes pretty well with her husband's green hair, don't you think?" Therefore, I've decided before the word becomes absolutely obsolete, I had better write about "Things that I find strange."

Living across the street from the "Police Station," and one block away from a very busy Fire Station, my ears have become very familiar with the sound of a siren. I have found the sound of a siren frightful, and disturbing, but I never considered it strange, until I looked the word up in a dictionary one day at work. I discovered the word comes from Greek mythology, of which a mythical story is told. I decided to write a story of my own, and discovered the definition of the word, holds a very strange paradox.

The Legend of the Siren

The night was still, as the large ship moved into the fog, which was making visibility virtually impossible. Many days had passed since the ships departure, when the valuable cargo had been loaded aboard. The captain's hands were wet from a fearful sweat, as he stood looking over the hull. It was not the fog that made him feel so fearful, he had sailed in fog many times. Nor was it the valuable cargo, for he had carried the treasures of a king in travels past. This journey was one he had dreaded for a long time, a trip, he had never made before. Many ships had ventured before him in these waters, never to be seen again. For the water they were in, passed by an island that had became a Greek legend. The captain's crew had heard the story many times.

On this island lived a group of nymphs (female divinities), who dwelled among the trees. According to the legend, they lured the sailors to destruction, by their sweet singing. They made the sound of a siren. Thus, the reason one of the definitions of the word siren is, "Fascinating dangerous women." When the sailors would hear this sound, they would direct their ship toward the island, which was surrounded by large dangerous rocks. Rocks, that would bring and end, to any ship that hit them. Thereby destroying the ship, leaving the crew to be fed to the creatures in the water.

This sound, the sound of a siren, was so irresistible it is told, that the sailors could not resist its pull, knowing of the destruction that would befall them. As it had done, to those who had met its fate before them. The temptation to destruction, by the sound of the siren, was so strong, the captain of the ship would have the crew tie each other to the ship, and then bind his own hands, to avoid steering the ship to its doom.

"I find it strange, that the sound of a siren, once brought destruction. Now destruction, brings the sound of a siren."

We are living in the days where knowledge has increased, and we have a better understanding of many things that must have made the natives absolutely crazy. Such as an "Eclipse." And while we still find this phenomenal event a bit strange, I discovered something "Stranger Than An Eclipse."

Stranger than an Eclipse

"A solar eclipse, the passage of the moon between the sun and the observer." It was Tuesday, May 10, 1994. Everyone was talking about the sun. It was going to do a strange thing, that only happens every so many years. As I was asking myself why everyone was so excited about seeing this event, I was informed by the receptionist where I work, that my daughter Kris who was living in St. Louis, was on line one, wanting to speak with me. I picked up the phone and went through the usual, "Hi, how are you doing?" and "I'm doing fine," then asked her why she was calling me at work. "The reason I called, is to ask if you are going to watch the eclipse today." She said with an enthusiastic tone in her voice. "It probably won't happen again in your life time," she added. As I pondered on the thought of my time running out, I told her I really had not thought about it, as it did not mean that much to me. The eclipse was having quite an effect on everyone else it seemed, so as the conversation came to a close, I told Kris I would consider going outside at the proper time, to see the eclipse.

As the time approached for this event to occur, I noticed people coming out of their work places at a panic pace. They had in their hands a piece of paper, with a small pin hole, and a piece of cardboard. Some of them, even had a magnifying glass or a camera. One of the employees I work with, who is a diabetic, had a doctor's appointment that morning to find out what he should or should not eat, to keep his sugar level safe. He had just returned to work, and was in the break room. I noticed his hands shaking viciously, as he was trying to open a box of raisins, an item the doctor must have recommended, I thought. I asked him if they told him what to eat, thinking he was going to eat the raisins, and he looked up at me and said, "I'm making a box to see the sun, I've got to hurry!" I walked back outside and now the crowd of people, which had grown even larger, were looking through boxes, both large one's and small one's. Their head was up inside of some of those boxes. Groups of people, standing in circles, to observe what? A small black dot, covering a small bright dot! They were even looking at the sidewalk, to see circles being made by the reflection of the sun, penetrating through the tree limbs.

It was at this point, I noticed how the birds were flying around in a wild fashion and making more than a normal amount of noise, as they looked down on the humans doing their thing. This troubled me, until I suddenly received a glimpse of the obvious. The birds thought the people were acting stranger than the sun. It was not the eclipse that troubled the birds, it was the people's response to this event in the sky, that troubled them so. I found myself in agreement with my feathered friends. The anticipation, the fascination, and the reaction of the people, was "Stranger Than An Eclipse."

I would like to close this column on a more serious note. A subject that has troubled me deeply. The subject is the great divide, the estrangement, that so often takes place in a relationship. When it happens, to those involved, it seems strange that such a thing could happen. It need not happen, however, if one would consider and remember the things I have included in this article, which was inspired by three small lines of words, form an old black and white movie.

"We need to talk."…"Some things are better left unsaid."…"If we don't talk, we will become strangers."

Let's Try Not to be Like Strangers Anymore

When you first met, talking was the least of your problems. There were so many things you wanted to know about each other. You had an unlimited supply of questions to ask, and answers to give. This communication strengthened your relationship.

Friendship turned to love, and embodied withing this love, there was friendship. You walked, talked, laughed and cried together. Thus, developed a trust, and your relationship was inseparable. Your undivided attention for each other, created a singleness of heart, evident to all, by your verbal and physical expressions. For how can one have communication, without some kind of expression? "It's written on your face," you could say. Knowing that something was wrong, something was right, whatever the something, it wasn't something that could be hid, in a dark cold heart. Your lives were filled with sharing, happiness and joy, sorrow and pain. One singleness of purpose, being shared by two people.

As time has a way of changing the face of the earth, it slowly, often without warning changes a relationship. Things are taken for granted, such as the sound of silence. Now two people, living under the same roof, having gone their separate ways, find silence, which at times was golden, the irony of their relationship. Emotion, held captive in the soul, makes a relationship a half, of what used to be a whole. You sit in wonder, "What went wrong?" Perhaps I can tell you why. A young tree planted, without water, in time will surely die. Communication is the thirst of the soul, that sprinkles the heart, and makes it grow.

"We need to talk."…"If we don't talk, we will become like strangers."…"Let's try not to be like strangers anymore."

38

What on God's Earth is Life About?

One must surely wonder, perhaps even shout,
What on God's earth life is all about.
The presidential scandal, the war in Iraq—
However can one handle the stress of such a weight?
With April soon approaching, tax time drawing near,
Now must I fear no food on my plate?
With each passing day revelations are made
Concerning the vices we tend to enjoy.
With a role of the dice we play the game,
Taking the gamble. Our hand we should have stayed.
Increasing in knowledge up there with the best
Where we are rewarded to cheat on the test.
One must surely wonder, perhaps even shout,
What on God's earth life is all about.
Is it war and taxes, what is good and what is not,
About what we have learned, or what we have forgot?
Taking chance at someone else's expense
By doing things that just don't make sense?
One must surely wonder, perhaps even shout,
What on God's earth life is all about.

39

We Lose, Gain as We Grow Older

There is something I have noticed as I take this fast train ride through my 50s. It is how a person keeps experiencing new things while growing old.

The thing that has been the most obvious is how one keeps losing things. You lose your hair, your teeth, eyesight, strength, vital body organs and, I'm confidant, dozens of other things if I could only remember. I think memory is one of those things.

I do remember that you lose friends you have known for a lifetime, and you look to see which ones every day in the paper.

Not all is lost, however. There are some things you gain, such as weight, cataracts, wrinkles and age spots along with aches and pains in places you didn't even know you had. Who knows, perhaps you didn't even have those places?

Yes, growing old is like a tree in the fall, shedding its beauty, preparing for winter. I don't like winter. Do you?

40

Visiting the Past with Old Friends and Gentle Places

What a joy, oh what a joy it is, to run into an old friend, an old school mate, I have not seen in a long time. In the last few months, this has been happening to me quite often. I suspect it is because they have been seeing my picture every month in my column, and now know what I look like forty years later in life. Even a greater joy it is to have them come up to me and say, "I have been wanting to tell you I really enjoy reading your column!"

I am proud of my old friends and school mates. Every one of them has done well, in my opinion. As we cross paths in life, exchanging a few words about where we have been, and what we are now doing, I am always led to reach for my old high school year books and lavish awhile in the past. Everyone looks a little older now, and they seem so much wiser. Their personalities however, are as a rule the same. What is hard to believe and understand, is how well we knew each other as friends and school mates, and how little we know about each other now. We have grown out of touch with one another. This does not mean, however, that we have stopped thinking or caring for each other, during the many years in between. Just let two of us meet by chance somewhere in our town, and feel the bond that we once shared so long ago. At least I know I feel it! And as we past the big 50, we find ourselves looking in the paper for those we once knew as a dear friend, who now have departed the sphere we walked on together. As we see their names appear one by one, we realize that page in the newspaper, is waiting for our name to be there someday.

I always wonder when I see an old friend on that page, if their dreams were fulfilled before saying good-bye to this life so many take for granted. Did they find their purpose in life, and make a great effort in pursuing it? I am amazed at the number of years that have past, and the many paths that I have taken, convinced they were the right ones, only to find they were not. It was in taking a sentimental journey to my past, that I found my future, just a short few years ago. Perhaps the same thing awaits for you.

Back to Your Future

What were your childhood dreams? I invite you to take a journey back in time, and recall what it was you loved to do, and most inspired to be someday. A time when your imagination was free to roam where it may, and you believed anything was possible. Take a journey to your past, it could be your future!

As a child, I wanted to be many things. Depending on what day of the week you asked me, I wanted to be a policeman, a fireman, a cowboy, or an Indian. We all have had these kind of ambitions in our past. I loved music, and seemed to have a natural talent or gift in this artistic field. In my journey to my past, after much meditation upon this time frame of my life, I remembered something I had long forgotten, or simply overlooked. Something that kept coming to the surface in every area of my life. I remembered my love for writing. More than anything else, I loved to write. Even in my music, it was writing songs that I enjoyed the most. I wrote poems, that made my English teachers proud; I wrote jokes, to hide the sadness in my soul; I wrote slogans, that obtained a place to be heard; and advertisements, that found their way into the newspaper to sell a product. All before the age of ten. The times I felt most alive, was when I was permitting my imagination to be creative, and I set it to words on a piece of paper. The real reward came, when I would find something I had written, in print, published, serving mankind in some small way. I had forgotten that feeling until recently, when I made a visit to my past, and decided to make it my future.

Enough about me. How about you? What was it you loved to do? What really made you feel alive, more than anything else? It may have been drawing a picture, making a flower arrangement, or nursing a pet back to health. You and you alone, can make this journey to your past. You are the only one who can determine if your past still holds your future. If it does, I say go for it! I did, and I'm glad!

Someone once wrote, "Young people want to talk about their future, because they have no past. Old people want to talk about their past, because they have no future." I have good news for you today. I think you can find your future in your past, and you're never too old to have a future. It may just be in order to fulfill those childhood dreams, a little wisdom had to be saved up, and a little more time to be found in one's day, before they could become a reality. Now if your older and wiser, and you find you have time to slow down, let me encourage you this day, to take a trip. A trip, "Back To Your Future."

It may be true, that old people want to talk about their past, and I think that's OK. They don't need to live there, but a visit once in awhile is a rewarding experience. Recently I made a trip to the basement and found one of those treasures we sometimes keep and wonder why, it inspired the following article, and now, if for no other reason, I am glad that I kept it!

Among My Souvenirs

As they sorted through the old shoe box, the past life, of the owner of the priceless possessions, began to unfold. Within was; a black and white photograph of a baby three months old, a beautiful baby, with long black hair, and beautiful eyes, that would make the Gerber baby food people sit at attention; a large dress pin, given to him by his grandmother, broken on the back fastening side, with large red stones on the face side. He had imagined them to be red rubies, and that someday he would be a wealthy man because of this pin; a watch face with a picture of a tractor on it. He had won it in a card game, which was played with his friends in the old neighborhood; a worn red ribbon, and also a blue one. These he received on play day at school, in the potato sack race; a four-leaf clover, which had been pressed in a book and had turned brown. Many times had he searched, for a four-leaf clover, before he had found it; and a piece of rosin, that had freshened the bow of his uncle's violin. As they searched a little further, a pocket knife was found, rusty with worn broken blades. But, it was his first pocket item, that was also carried by his dad.

An old, red mill tax token, was then taken from the box, which was used when he was a child. It was there to remind him that there was such a thing, as a plastic tax token. They next picked up a wooden nickel, from a bicentennial celebration, the time his dad grew a beard to win a contest called, "Brothers Of The Brush." They also found; a single, white dice, which once belonged to the pair that rolled, "seven and eleven", twenty times in a roll, and won him a one dollar bet; a rugged piece of clay, which used to be some great artistic thing, he made as a child. Another picture found, was of his grandfather. The first uniform police officer in his town, wearing his steel helmet and holding a bully club. Also within was; a newspaper clipping of a poem he wrote, when he was ten years old; and a silver tarnished spoon, because it looked like grandma's spoon. The last item found was a tie clip, with a picture of a guitar on it. Perhaps symbolic of a childhood dream, to play such an instrument in a recording studio, that had become a reality.

The entire box of items, would not bring a dollar at an auction, I reckon. But these would be the things, "Among My Souvenirs."

41

Wind Ensemble Delights Audience

Once again I was enthralled by the wonderful music and talent of the Symphonic Wind Ensemble and its conductor, Robert Gifford. The Oct. 13 performance was another piece of excellence. For almost an hour I was about to forget about the presidential scandal and economic woes which are in the news each day and be immersed in the wonderful musical selections that were presented. I am always bewildered by the lack of attendance at these concerts. Nevertheless, this did not hinder the enthusiasm and heartfelt effort made by the members of the wind ensemble. This did not surprise me, however, as passion and ebullience are the chief characteristics of Gifford, the conductor. My thanks to the Southeast Missouri State University department of music for making this happening available to our community.

42

Sounds of Fall Provide Reminder

It's a beautiful Saturday morning. I am sitting on the weathered wooden planks of my back porch. The cool morning breeze is a gentle reminder that the fall season is near.

As I look forward to the east, I observe the rising of that lucky old sun. It has hearkened the call of a rooster who is crowing somewhere nearby. As the red brilliance of the sun rises over the muddy brown waters of the Mississippi, I hear the sound of a train rushing down the rails which run parallel with the river front. The clanging sound of the train wheels and its whistle blowing at each crossing, brings back memories of my grandfather who was once a conductor on such a train.

As I look toward the west, I see three birds perched on top of a utility pole, singing their praises to the Lord, I suppose. It must be eight o'clock as the bells of St. Mary's are ringing. How faithful are these bells each morning.

The church, which is in full view as I look toward the south, is one of the great landmarks in my neighborhood. It has been a historic symbol which has brought back memories of my past back to life, as has the funeral home which is in the path between the church and my house. The funeral home is now a daily reminder that life on this earth is but temporal, and the church is a daily reminder that for those who trust in God, life is eternal.

43

Let's Go to the Movies

My earliest recollection of attending the movies was when I was around the age of seven or eight. Mom and Dad would always take us kids along with them to the movies. I especially remember us walking to the theater, us kids in front, mom and dad close behind, strolling up Sprigg Street to Broadway. My mom would always ask, "Ronnie, do you have to go to the bathroom?" I of course would reply, "No!," even though I was feeling an urgent need to relieve a gallon of Kool-Aid. What amazed me was, how did she always know? Now as I look back on that walk, with me stopping ever so often, with my legs tightly crossed and squeezed together, I guess it didn't take a genius to at least suspect I had a problem.

Keeping Me on My Knees

When we arrived at the Rialto or Broadway Theater, we would all sit down together toward the back, to enjoy the show. My brother and I never sat very long, however. Once the movie began, we would get up to go to the rest room, and then begin, what became a very profitable way to make money. Enough money to buy soda and candy to our hearts delight. Our first venture into this new activity, came one night after I received what I thought to be a brilliant idea. I said to my brother, "Hey Danny, lets get down on our knees, crawl down the center isle, and see if we can find any change on the floor." I thought perhaps someone might have a hole in their pocket, or just accidentally had dropped a nickel or a dime. So the two of us, him on one side, and I on the other, quietly crawled from the back to the front, on our knees looking for some loose change. Sure enough, we both found enough for a treat. Having this success the very first time, the movie didn't matter anymore. We decided to try it again. This time, we would stay together. Just maybe, what one of us overlooked, the other would find. Down the isle we went, this time not so quietly, as we kept giggling every time we found a coin. We did even better the second time around than we did on the first trip we made! This became a rewarding experience for us, until mom discovered what we were doing and made us quit. I have often wondered how we were able to find so much money on the floor. I can't go to a movie today without looking down on the floor, thinking I might find a few coins. I've come to believe the reason we always found coins on the floor for us to spend, was due to the kind people who were dropping coins for us to find. I suppose they did this for one of the following reasons. Either so we could have a treat, or to keep us out of their feet and to be quiet, until the movie was over.

A few years later, one would still find me going to the movies, for reasons other than watching them.

A Kiss Is Just a Kiss

By the age of ten, I was going to the movies on my own. I was making money to spend, and I enjoyed spending it on the candy and even chewing gum one could buy at the refreshment center. I really enjoyed, Black Jack Gum, a licorice flavored gum that was popular during that time.

One Saturday afternoon, while at the movies chewing that gum, I saw a pretty little girl, around my age, sitting on the front row. I walked down front, sat down beside her, and acted like I was enjoying the show. I introduced myself to her, then asked her if she had ever been kissed. She replied that she had most certainly not. I told her that I had, "As a matter of fact," I said, "I have been kissed quite a bit by a girl, an older girl." Now this was true. My older sister had a friend named Cora Lee, who practiced kissing on me, "Instead of a fence post," she said. "I enjoyed it, Cora Lee!" Just in case your reading this. Anyway, back to the girl on the front row. I asked her, "Would you like to be kissed?" She said, "OK." So I quickly gave her a peck on her little lips, which was followed by her saying, "Ugh!" I was shocked at her response, and I asked her what was wrong. She said I tasted like licorice. I suppose I learned a lesson or two that day. If you're going to kiss a girl, make sure they like your breath, and whenever possible, save your kissing for the older girls, they seem to be more experienced at it.

Movie houses were certainly different back in those days. On bargain night, for the price of a quarter, or a dime, one could see two full length movies with cartoons in between. Even as I entered my teens, it was fifty cents I believe, to see a top-rated movie. Movies didn't receive ratings in those days, they didn't need to. It was the activity going on during the movies, however, that should have been rated. Proper conduct in theaters has certainly improved in recent years, as the conduct on the screen has diminished.

It wasn't uncommon to have a special celebrity to come to one of the theaters. I remember seeing Gabby Hayes one time at the Rialto. I got his photo and autograph. Do you remember Gabby Hayes? Once at the Broadway theater, they had on a Friday the 13th, "The return of James Dean." Word was, he might just come back to life for all the young girls who loved him if they would show up. They showed up for sure, but no James Dean. I went to see just how stupid it would be, and to see the girls have their hearts broke. Perhaps I could help mend them afterwards. Over the years, movies became better in some ways with the new technology and bright new actors. The introduction of color was of course super. But with the introduction of the VCR and video stores, where one can rent a movie and view it in the privacy of their home, I'm surprised that movie houses still exist.

I'll See You After the Show

As a matter of fact, I've been watching a movie with my wife, on our VCR, and I am taking a popcorn break to tell you about movies your family should consider, for family viewing. The movie we are watching is, "Mr. Smith Goes To Washington." This movie is from the Columbia Classic Studio Heritage Collection. The film, starring Jimmy Stewart and Jean Arthur, won eleven nominations (including Best Picture and Best Director), and winning one (Best Motion Picture Story). Jimmy Stewart, who portrays Mr. Smith, finds himself elected to the senate, and is sent to Washington. He finds his image of the city, full of politicians, with the character of Abe Lincoln, to be a misguided one. Instead he finds himself single-handedly battling ruthless politicians, who are out to destroy him. The plot of the movie is not what I wish to tell you about, however.

Recently, someone wrote a book called, "Raising PG kids in a X Rated Society." I never bought the book, but I can guess what it has to say. The movies that are being produced today, must contain certain ingredients to be a success. Why? Will somebody please tell me why? Why a movie must show some skin, with sex scenes that make the devil blush. Why? Why must a movie have a vocabulary, with four letter foul words in every other sentence or every other word? Why? Why must there be killing and blood, cheating and stealing, and every other commandment the Lord gave, broken before our eyes, and fed into our ears to hear? Why? They say the reason is, it makes a good movie. I say, a good movie is one that contains none of the above.

Movies, such as "Mr. Smith Goes To Washington", are entertaining, delightful, funny, and keep you sitting on the edge of your seat. They also have within them a lesson worth learning. A good moral lesson you would want your children and grandchildren to learn. They contain none of the filth being instilled in the movies of the nineties, and were never considered for a rating, not even a PG rating. Movies such as these, should be promoted and encouraged, and that's what I am doing now.

The Columbia Classics Studio Heritage Collection, represents a commitment to the preservation of popular film culture, through a painstaking restoration effort. Each time you purchase one of these films you support this cause. I am not trying to sell movies, I am trying to get people to go back to watching movies, that were presentable and moral enough for the entire family to watch together. Perhaps, this is one of the reasons for the breakdown in the family structure. Once upon a time, families watched movies together. What was good enough for the kids, was good enough for mom and dad. When did we lose this wonderful part of our lifestyle? In the meantime, "I'll See You After The Show."

44

It's Time for Some National Hoopla

I have been thinking about this milking the cow thing, better known as Milkgate. I believe we are going to really miss the jersey if we don't milk this cow for all it's worth.

I see great potential for our city to reap huge benefits from this windfall. We could become famous for being known as the city that milks the cow. Song No. 11, "Milk Cow Blues Boogie," on Bill Swan's new CD, would become a No. 1 hit. Local folks would be asked to appear in television advertisements drinking a glass of milk, some with their left hand and some with their right.

People across America will be wearing T-shirts which ask the question, "Do you milk a cow from the left or the right?" One of our milk cows could become a celebrity right along with Melvin Gateley. I can even see a book in the works: "The Day the Milk Cow Died," a novel about a town that became prosperous overnight from publicity about a milking contest and the debate that followed.

Then the book becomes a movie. It is as big as "Titanic." Wow! I can't stand any more of this fantasizing. I think I have been reading too many of Steve Mosley's letters to the editor. It's scary. I am beginning to think and write like Steve. How could something like this ever happen?

It's probably those aliens from outer space Steve's been talking about. They put his strange creativity in my brain. Before I lose it all, permit me to make this famous quote: "Left ain't right, and right ain't wrong."

45

God Takes Control, Heals Addiction

When I was seven years old, I witnessed God's supernatural power in a personal way. It was then that I first became aware of God's hand on my life.

It was 12 years later, after traveling many different roads searching for happiness and peace, that God once again supernaturally intervened in my life. The Lord showed me that peace and joy are found in trusting in him and his Word.

Nevertheless, the world has a way of distracting one from this truth. Soon I was on the road again, looking for the love only God can give. I reached a point in my life where I vowed I would never be. I became an alcoholic.

I was about to lose my family and my job. At the age of 38, I had reached a bridge in my life with the choice of living or dying. God provided me the opportunity to make that choice in a supernatural way.

The choice I made was to live and have a personal relationship with the Lord. On Aug. 1, 1981, I was completely healed of my addiction. I have since served the Lord with all my heart and have used the talents he has given me to the best of my ability.

46

A Child's Day Off from School

On cold winter mornings, shortly after the moon had tucked in, and the sun had made it out of the cover of darkness, my mom would wake four very sleepy eyed children, to greet another day. I, being one of them, would sit up in bed, and observe the frozen ice on the window, not yet yielding to the warmth of the sun's reflection. In a very rapid fashion, the four of us, would grab our clothes for the day, then quickly make a circle hugging the old coal stove in our living room, which was the only room that had heat. After getting dressed, we would answer mom's call to come for breakfast. Mom would always have a hot bowl of oats waiting for us, serving it up with toast, and letting us add all the sugar and butter we needed to make it taste the way we wanted it to. This took off the chill on the inside, of once cold bodies it seemed, and we would be ready at this point to meet the day. In the winter, this meant going to school. The school had radiator heat, and it was a good heating system. However, the radiators became very warm, and almost hot, to the touch of a small child's hand.

On this particular day, it would be my first attempt to pretend I was sick, so I could leave school and be sent home. I told my teacher I was sick at my stomach, and that I felt like I was going to puke. When she took me to the school nurse and told the nurse what I had said, the nurse immediately scolded me for using the word puke. She told me it was improper, vulgar, and that I should never ever use that word again. I asked her what word would be proper, and she informed me I should say "vomit." Now personally, I don't like either of these words. I didn't like them then, and I don't like them now. However, for purposes of getting out of school, a child must choose one of them, and preferably choose the word most suitable for the nurse. Perhaps then, at least, she will have a heart of pity, when you say you are sick. Back to my conversation with the nurse. She began asking me questions like she was "Mrs. Perry Mason," raising her eyebrow every time I put my hand on my stomach and made a pitiful moan. I always leaned in her direction when doing so, wondering if she wanted that nice white uniform to be spoiled for the day. "Let's see if you have any fever," she said, sticking the thermometer in my mouth. "I'll be right back," she barked, as she left the room, to tell the principal most likely, that I was trying to get out of school by playing sick.

Now I was young, really young, probably first or second grade. Nevertheless, I was smart enough to know, that the only way I was going to convince this nurse that I had any fever, was to get that thing she put in my mouth really hot! So, I decided to lay it on the radiator and let it warm up until she came back. She was gone much longer than I thought she would be. Perhaps, she was hoping I would give up this act and return to class. Finally, I heard her walking toward the door, so I grabbed the thermometer and quickly inserted it in my mouth. In doing so, I found it was so hot, it burned my tongue and made me cry. I knew I couldn't take it out, or she would realize what I had done. She opened the door to a small teary eyed child, and reached for the thermometer. As she removed it she let out a scream. I thought she had burned her fingers, but with fear in her voice, she told me I had the highest fever she had ever seen in a child. The expression on her face reflected only concern for my health, and perhaps a little guilt for not believing me when I told her I was sick. Now it was I, who was feeling more than a little bit of guilt, for pretending I was sick when I wasn't. She said, "I want you to tell your mother as soon as you get home, to take you to the doctor immediately!" I promised her that if I was still hot when I got home, I would.

Adding a little to the drama I was performing, I said in an emotional tone, "Perhaps that cold winter air will cool my poor hot head, and I will feel better when I get home." When I arrived home, my mom was in disbelief that the school had sent me home. "All I know is that the nurse said I was sick, but I really feel fine now!" I told my mom.

So what does a child do, when he has been sent home from school? For one thing, you try to stay out of your mom's way! In doing this, I found the attic and the basement both interesting places to venture.

In the attic, I found items left by the previous resident, such as carved wooden picture frames, old books, and some old canceled and blank checks, from a bank which was no longer in existence. Thus, I could write myself a check with as many zeros as I wished, pretending I was a wealthy man living in a mansion. With a little imagination, I could visualize works of great art in those picture frames, and rarity in those dusty old books. And it all belonged to me!

Then there was the basement, dark, damp, cold, with a huge pile of black rocks, which made that stove in our living room hot. Thinking about the basement now, it seems it would have been a very dreary place to be, but back then, it was quite interesting for some strange reason. Perhaps, it was because we had bats in our basement. The flying kind! They never frightened me, but I was concerned at times that they might fly into my hair. They were like airplanes without radar, flying in the dark, having no direction or particular destination.

When time for school to be over finally arrived, I knew it was safe to go outside. I would play with our cat "Inky" for a while, then walk over to Mr. Maier's station on the corner of William and Sprigg. I wanted to show him something that I had written. I had been writing poems and jokes for quite sometime, but this was something special, I had written an advertisement for him to submit to the newspaper. When I handed it to him, he was very pleased.

As I recall, he gave me a dime and a nickel, and told me to get me a soda pop and candy. There was a bright red Coke machine and a tall green candy machine inside his station, that I often used. Thus, I became a professional writer, definition being "One who gets paid", during my first years of grade school. I haven't been paid since! Mr. Maier was a really nice person for kids to be around. I spent countless hours telling him my tall tales, and with great patience and interest, he listened. Young people need someone who will listen, even if that person is a store clerk, or an employee of some other sort of business, something we need to remember.

After visiting with Mr. Maier, I headed for Good Hope street, stopping along the way to visit with the Haas sisters, Antonia, and Aletha. I always stopped at their house on my way to Good Hope. Antonia called me her little boy friend, and most of the time, she had a bright shiny quarter for me to spend at Hirch's Grocery. Hirch's Grocery brings back enough memories to write an article about. Such as the time I saw in person Aunt Jemima, the lady on the syrup bottle, and I met the Philip Morris man, a short little guy, who shouted with a loud voice, "Call for Philip Morris." After spending my Quarter, Antonia so generously gave me, I would head back to the house, stopping along the way to talk to Charlie, who lived across the street form the Haas sisters. He too, gave me some pocket change most of the time, but this was never the reason I stopped and visited with my friends on my way to Good Hope. I felt like they needed someone to talk to. I never met a stranger, and I enjoyed talking, but more important, I enjoyed listening to people! How sad it is that today we find it not safe for little ones to talk to strangers.

Upon returned home, I would finish out this day off, by sitting in front of the large Philco radio, listening to "The shadow", "Amos and Andy", and other great radio shows, where ones imagination created the pictures, to go with the dreams they were listening to. Ask anyone who remembers living in those days, and see if they would have traded them for the present. I know I certainly wouldn't!

47

Three Years of Column Writing

I wish to invite your readers to make a special effort to read TBY: The Best Years which will be in Monday's paper. I have countless people tell me they enjoy what I write. Sometimes they are referring to a letter to the editor. Sometimes they are referring to my column, "Written From the Heart," in TBY. The upcoming column marks my third year of writing for TBY, and I think this column may be a collector's item. In fact, I have been thinking about what I might do to make this column a rarity that people would stand in line for. Some of the ideas:

1. Include a serial number at the end of the column for identification purposes.

2. Create a shortage by buying as many papers on TBY day as I can afford.

3. Talk Steve Mosley into sharing his close encounter of a different kind in a limited edition.

I suppose the thing that would work the best to make my column a rarity would be for me to quit writing it. Believe me, I've tried. Every time I give it serious consideration, someone tells me or calls Speak Out saying how much he enjoys my column. I would like to take this opportunity to say thank you to those of you who have done so.

48

Dirt Hauling Trucks Disturb Sleep

Last Saturday evening, many folks paid good money to hear the sound of monster trucks at the Show Me Center, leaving them with ringing ears and headaches beyond belief. Not I. I went to bed at a decent hour so I would feel like going to church on Sunday.

I was awakened before midnight by the sound of monster trucks right outside my house. The show must be over, I thought, and the trucks are heading home. When midnight approached and my windows were still shaking, I got out of bed to see how big these monster trucks were. To my surprise, the parade of trucks passing by my house included huge dump trucks loaded with dirt. They were making a left turn off Sprigg Street and onto Merriwether Street, the block on which I live, to dump off the dirt somewhere at the end of the block, and then returning for another load. They kept coming and going, shifting gears, pounding their brakes and making the sound of their engines rise to a level louder than a "Rush" concert I once attended in St. Louis with my son.

I called the police station. The lady who took my call said she was unaware there were any trucks. I said, "You mean to tell me you can't hear these trucks?" She replied, "It's so noisy in here we can't hear anything outside."

I continued to listen and watch this free monster-truck show until after 1 a.m., thinking it would soon come to an end. It didn't. I called the police station again and explained I was ready to go back to bed and wanted the noise from the trucks to cease. She had an officer speak with me about my problem. He informed me the trucks were hauling dirt from the Show Me Center, dirt that had been used at the show the previous evening. He said the dirt had to be out before morning, and there was nothing he or I could do about it.

I informed him that I was amazed that an officer would be sent after receiving a call about loud noise from an apartment complex or that the police would pull over a car with a boom box making excessive noise. However, these trucks could parade in front of my home between the hours of midnight and 2 a.m. making the noise I have previously described.

Living across the street form the police station and one block away from the fire station, I have learned to ignore the sounds of sirens. I have done so without any remorse, as I know they are necessary. I am hard pressed, however, to see the necessity of hauling dirt at a time when people need a good night's sleep.

49

Would Christmas Have Been a Forgotten Holiday?

You hear it every year. "Isn't it sad, how Christmas has became so commercialized? Yes, they have even went so far, as to take Christ out of the word Christmas. Worst still, they have replaced it with an x, can you believe it? Not only have they removed Christ from Christmas, they have replaced him with a character whose name is Santa Claus. Every year the stores try to start the Christmas season earlier. Can you believe Christmas in July?"

Is Christmas just for Christians? Just for church denominations, and those who favor the Lord, by remembering that he does exist on Sunday? Has the world given Christmas a bad name? I once thought that it was just for Christians, and that the world had indeed, disgraced this blessed holiday.

As a child, I found the emphasis placed on this day, was Santa Claus, and the presents he would bring. It was always a joyful time, when fruit and a variety of nuts were in abundance in our home. An event that only took place this time of the year. I raised my children in the same manner. They would look with excitement and anticipation, for Christmas morning to arrive, to see if the cookies and milk were eaten or drank and to see the presents left under the Christmas tree they had decorated. When my youngest child discovered from his school mates, that mom and dad had him believing in a fairy tale, he was more than disappointed. Not only by the fact that his friends were correct, but disappointed, in mom and dad! This got me to thinking about the error of my ways.

Had I belittled the most important holiday of the year? Yes, I had, was my answer. Santa Claus was wrong, and I was not placing the emphasis on Christ. I became an enemy of Santa. Then, I became a protester of anyone who commercialized this holiday. Why didn't the world just leave this holiday alone and let us Christians enjoy it, became my thinking.

Then one day, just prior to the Christmas season, this thought came to my heart and mind. What if, the world suddenly stopped giving special prominence to this day? By a government decree, no longer would the world give commercial emphasis for the Christmas season. What would be the impact of such a happening? How would the unsaved, who have vowed to never enter the door of a building called a place of worship, ever be reminded that on December 25th, we celebrate the birth of their savior, as well as ours? For what reason would the stores have, to encourage the spirit of giving to others, as they give unto you? How would the "lost sheep of this world" ever hear, when shopping in the mall, the songs of the child, born in a manger, who became the King of Kings? Never again would cars in December drive down their city streets, and be reminded of the birth of the Christ, by the decorations stretched out overhead. There wouldn't be the manger scenes, nor Christmas trees, nor stockings by the bed. Would our children, still look with anticipation to this day, where the joy of receiving is only exceeded by the joy of giving? In the dead of winter, due to the climate and the harsh weather, jobs are hard to find and expenses run so high. Would there be a need of additional part time employees to sell merchandise, if there were no Christmas season? Would our children still hear Christmas carols, and have Christmas programs in their schools? As a final but scary thought, would our church's maintain the spirit of Christmas, if the commercial world had not kept it alive? Would Christmas have been a forgotten holiday? Perhaps, we should not be so critical of the commercial aspect of Christmas. It may well be, that this has been a great witness unto the world. If the world wants to promote and encourage our Savior's birth, and its only hope, let us not prevent it by complaining. Let us encourage it by our support, always being mindful that "Jesus, is the reason for the season!"

I have left room in my column to share with you a poem I so wanted to share last Christmas. It was written just for you, as my way of saying, "Merry Christmas!"

Snowing in Manassas a Christmas Story

It has been snowing for days in Manassas. With Christmas only a few days away, it looked to be a white Christmas that year. But for some, as it so often is, it was looking like a blue Christmas.

For an unwed teenager, with her baby a few days old, who wanted to come home for Christmas, to parents unaware of her plight. It was looking like a blue Christmas.

For a mother of three small children, who had lost her husband and now lost her job, just days before Christmas. All the snow in Manassas, could not cover the blue she was feeling this season. It was looking like a blue Christmas.

And for the young couple, who ran a café in Manassas. Married for five years, unable to have a much wanted child and still waiting to adopt one. If for one day, Christmas day, to feel the joy of having a child. Hanging the ornaments on their Christmas tree, with no child to enjoy the tree with them, was like an unanswered prayer. Wrapped in blue, tied in blue, it was looking like a blue Christmas.

Perhaps the café should be open on Christmas day, and they should take the tree there for others to enjoy. After all, they had been very busy with all the Christmas shoppers, coming in for a sandwich or a nice cup of hot chocolate. They had been so busy in fact, they were wishing they had hired someone to wait on tables, at least until after the holidays...

Twas the night before Christmas and in their café, sat a mother of three, her hair slightly grey.

And a young teenage girl, just wanting to rest. While she fed her new infant, milk from her breast.

She cried out, "I want to go home, but I don't know how." The mother of three said, "I saw your help-wanted sign, I need a job, I can start right now!"

The young café owners, looked at her in dismay, for there was no such sign on display.

The teenager looking at them desperately, shouted out the following plea.

"Could you keep my baby, just for tonight, so I can explain to my parents, my previous plight?"

The young couple said, "If we had someone to run our café, in our home tonight the baby could stay."

"I will run your café," said the mother of three, "I need a job, how about me?"

So the young café owners on Christmas day, had a young infant, to cuddle and play.

The teenager had time to express verbally, of her plight to the joyful grandparents to be.

The mother of three on Christmas day, while waiting on tables cheerfully, met a father for her children and her new husband to be.

It's snowing in Manassas, blue is turning white. Merry Christmas to all, and to all a good night!

50

Dream Brings Three Possibilities

I recently had a dream. In this dream, I observed the planet Earth revolving around like a spinning ball. Standing in the center of the planet was an object like a statue. This object had everyone's attention. While observing the object, I heard voices shouting out all of the woes and problems which the Earth is facing. The voices were coming from different geographical areas on the globe, and the sound of the voices and the pleas they were voicing were being ignored. Everyone was so engulfed in this object that held their attention that all else had become obscured. When I awoke from this dream, I was amazed that an object could distract people from such serious problems as the world is facing. I thought about this dream for days, wondering if it contained a message one should consider or if it was from drinking too much chocolate milk before going to bed. I thought of three things which the statue may have represented, two things which have had the nation in their grip, and one thing which may be the only salvation for our nation's survival.

The statue may have represented the attention which has been given to Mark McGwire. The Missourian said it best on the front page of Sunday's edition: "Americans once again this year turned their attention to baseball in a season that will go down in history as one of the best ever." I am proud of McGwire and what he has done. I think he comes as close as anything we have seen in a long time to being a hero. And I think he has eased the pain somewhat of the second thing the statue may have been.

The statue may have represented the attention which has been given to Bill Clinton. His actions have brought forth a cloud of darkness over our nation. For him, the statue represents his dilemma as to how he can remain in office. While the problems of the world cry out to be heard and addressed, he must focus on how to tell the next lie and get by with it. For us, the statue represents how hungry we have become for tabloid news to intervene in someone's personal life.

The third thing the statue may have represented is the person we should be giving our attention to in a time such as this. That person is Jesus Christ. With the world in turmoil and its leadership weakened, the need to keep your focus on Jesus has become what one would think would be obvious. He alone has the answer to the problems the world faces. While Clinton may still sit in the White House, the Lord still sits on his throne.

51

Bob King's Music Will Last Forever in Heavenly Home

With each passing year, I am saddened by the loss of dear friends with whom I have shared my great love for music.

Bob King was at the top of the list of these dear friends, as was his wife, Geneva. I played lead guitar on stage with Bob many a weekend while crowds enjoyed his talent on the violin as he played a beautiful waltz.

My first memory of the three of us playing music was a practice session we had in Bob's home—Bob with his fiddle, Geneva on the piano and I with my guitar. We were playing "Just a Closer Walk With Thee." We each took turns playing the melody, and we were enjoying ourselves so much we did not want the song to end.

I and many others will miss Bob, who performed his music with such a passion. Nevertheless, I am filled with joy knowing that Bob is now living that song, "Just a Closer Walk With Thee." This time the song will never end.

52

The Best Years

The best years, 40+! A time in one's life, where you come to the realization of some undeniable truths. After wandering in the wilderness of life for forty years, wisdom has finally arrived, and now you are heading for the promise land! I have made some interesting observations of changes that occur, beginning at the age of forty or there about.

Time, Where Did It Go?

I remember one sunny afternoon, while I was collecting water samples at a land field, I observed two jets flying overhead performing exercises. Out of no where the jets would suddenly appear, and just as suddenly, they would disappear. I kept saying, "Here comes one!" Followed by, "Where did it go?" This happens to the years when you reach forty. On life's roller coaster, you get on board, starting at the bottom for a long slow ride. A climb which takes forty years before reaching the peak, you begin the down hill slide, picking up speed as you go. Years soon pass at the speed of light, "Here comes one, Where did it go?" These are your best years, and they last about the same amount of time it takes to watch a movie. Thus, most of your memories are of the first forty years of your life. You find yourself holding on to these years like a precious jewel, taking it with you on your journey.

The Body, Where Did It Go?

"I have often wondered, where all of my old school mates moved off to. I have now come to realize, they haven't moved, they are living in the best years."

I recently looked at some old photos of "yours truly," when I was in my teens and right after I got married, around mid-twenties. It will be a long time before I repeat this act of self inflicted depression again!

When a person reaches the best years, 40+, something happens to the body, Actually, many things happen to the body. One of these things is weight gain. Some call it middle age spread, or excessive baggage. Call it whatever you will, it happens! At least to the majority of us. You know it is true! Eat a sweet roll or a piece of cake in a dark closet, and everyone you run into that day will know that you ate it, just by observing the weight you instantly gained, when you partook of that sinful thing. Once upon a time, before your best years, you could eat to your hearts desire, and never gain a pound. Now, you just look at food and you will gain a pound. It's carrot sticks and salads for us now. These are the best years.

Vitality, Where Did It Go?

There are three types of people who walk in the mall: (1) Teenagers, walking to see who they might just run into. (2) Young married adults, walking with little children, holding their hands, while they try to stretch the dollar, as much as the little ones have stretched their budget. (3) The "best year" people. Walking because our skin is stretching and drooping, and our hearts are lagging as we gasp for a breath of air.

When you reach the best years, you may very well have a position in life that requires little physical effort. Now you can use your wisdom and gained knowledge, to make a living, instead of hard labor. The lack of exercise on a daily routine, soon robs us of our energy, and we find ourselves buying exercise machines we never use, or walking at the mall. It's the "use it or lose it" principle. This principle pertains to all things, you will discover, when your living in the best years.

Money, Where Did It Go?

If you are currently living in the best years, you are living with the "Ten Factor." You grew up paying ten to fifty cents to go to the movies. You can remember buying a gallon a gas for a dime, during the gas wars. A soda pop was a nickel or a dime, with a two-cent refund on the bottle. A hamburger was a quarter, and so was a chocolate shake. It is hard to get these prices out of your mind, once you have experienced them. So, you give your child a five-dollar bill, and tell them to have fun filled evening. They begin it with a meal at a fast food restaurant, and come back for more money. "Where did the money go?" You ask. You ask because you are living with the "Ten Factor." Your living in a time where everything cost ten times as much as it did before you entered the best years.

Conclusion

I must wonder, are we who have surpassed the age of forty, living in the best years? One thing is certain, they can be the best years. Life, is pretty much what we make it to be. Nevertheless, I tend to believe, those of us who were born in the early forties or fifties, were brought up in the best years. A time when food was real, the music was earth shaking, not deaf making, and prosperity and security appeared in our future to behold. Ron Duff, a dear friend of mine, described this quite well when we crossed paths at a fast food restaurant not long ago. While looking at the menu trying to decide what to order, he said to me, "Ron, life just isn't simple anymore! There are too many choices to make about everything, even buying a hamburger. It wasn't like this when we were growing up." My friend, Ron, was so right! Life was simple then. If you wanted a hamburger, you just asked for one. Today, we have dozen different kinds of hamburgers we must choose from. Think about it! If you needed gas for your car, your choice was regular. Today, you must choose from three grades of unleaded. If you had a headache or fever, you got an aspirin. How many types of pain relievers are there to select from today? A trip to the grocery store can drive one crazy. We have "Fat Free, Salt Free, No Fat, Less Fat, Regular, Light, or Extra Light." The list goes on and on.

For Ron and I, the years of our youth were good years, if not "the best years." This is not to say, however, that the years we are living in are not good years, and may become the best years. We have seen our children become adults, and now, we can experience the joy of being a grandparent. We can look back and see the progress the world has made, and see the mistakes that have been as well. Having more knowledge and a little more wisdom, one can perceive the foolishness of seeking material gain, at the expense of happiness, and the short amount of time one has on this planet. Life is but a vapor, and we are but passing through, as visitors on this planet. Visiting here to learn and to spread a message of love, all in preparation for "the best years," soon to come!

53

A Prayer to Help Others

Here is a prayer my wife and I have found to be helpful when we pray for others: Dear Lord, help me search my heart for any unconfessed sin. If there is any sin within me, I confess that sin now, knowing that you are faithful and just to forgive my sins and cleanse me from all unrighteousness.

Create in me a clean heart, O God, and renew a right spirit within me, by the blood of Jesus Christ, who cleanses us from all sin. I thank you, Lord, for forgiving my sins and placing them in the sea of forgiveness where they will surface no more nor be remembered by you.

Thank you, Father, for sending your son, who purchased us with his blood. For in him we have redemption and the forgiveness of sins. And, by his blood, we are justified.

I thank you, Lord, that I can come boldly before your throne of grace and enter into your presence where I can give you thanks and praise your holy name. How precious is your name. Because you have given me the spirit of adoption, I can call you Father.

You are the good shepherd who leads me beside the still waters. You are my almighty God, my everlasting father, my deliverer and my shield. It is in you I take refuge. You are the strength of my life. You are the Lord that healeth. You are the way, the truth and the life, the beginning and the end. Because of your love for me, you had mercy on my soul and called me with a holy calling. I give you praise.

You have redeemed me from the curse of the law. It is you, and you alone, who forgives our iniquities, heals our diseases, redeems our lives from destruction and crowns us with your loving kindness and tender mercies. You have made us more than conquerors through him who loves us and who has given us the victory. All this we obtained through our Lord Jesus Christ.

Thank you for hearing my prayers and for your promise that you will be listening and answering them before I call upon your name.

Teach me to make my prayers more effective, and stir up the gift within me so my prayers will be fervent and will availeth much. Help all who are praying in intercession in one accord to know that we still receive what we ask for as you have promised.

Let not my will but thy will be done this day as I make my heart silent before you. May the Holy Spirit show me what and for whom I should pray as he makes intercession for me according to your will.

54

Mirrors Are Faulty

I wish someone would tell me why they don't make mirrors like they used to. I can remember once when mirrors were honest. When I looked at that mirror, it reflected my handsome, slim body, my dark brown hair, the color of my eyes and my teeth. Have they changed the type of glass or the process for making mirrors? I wonder.

These new mirrors, right at about my waistline, seem to be warped or something. Actually, the entire mirror seems defective. It makes my skin look wrinkled. And my dark brown hair? Can you believe that mirror has given it shades of gray? Mirrors are not as clear as they used to be either. The image has become so faint on these new mirrors I can hardly see my eyes, much less detect the color of them. And my teeth? It seems they don't appear at all any more for some reason.

If you know where I can get a mirror that will reflect my body as it once did 30 years ago, please get in touch with me.

55

A Matter of the Heart

Back in the late fifties or early sixties, late one evening, we loaded the one car with all our band equipment. Larry and Paul, Louis and myself, along with Chuck and Bill, squeezed in the car, and headed for Memphis Tennessee.

We were making Larry's first recording in a real recording studio, and we had to be in the recording studio early in the morning.

We were unable to sleep, excited about making the recording, so we decided to get to Memphis early, drive to Elvis Presley's mansion, and park the car in front of it. Perhaps we would get to see him coming in late at night in his big Cadillac.

When we arrived at his place, we parked almost directly in front of the gates. A huge flood light in his front yard, kept flashing on our car, and I was just sure the police would be arriving any moment, but they didn't.

Suddenly, sure enough, a long Cadillac pulled up in front of the gates which quickly opened. We all sat up to see Elvis, and saw his father instead.

He looked very much like Elvis, and we were delighted just to see him.

Feeling the pangs of hunger, we decided it was time to try to find some place open where we could grab a bite of breakfast.

As we drove into the downtown section of the city, it was still too early for food places to be open, with the exception of one place which appeared to be getting ready to open.

With the lights being on, we decided to venture in, and ask the colored cook if we could sit and wait till he was ready to serve breakfast.

He looked at us like we were crazy and said, "Are you sure you want to eat here?" Being that there was no other place even appearing as if they were going to open soon and since he was heating up his grill, we replied, "Sure, perhaps you could get us a cup of coffee."

This he did, still looking at us in a mighty strange way, as he brought us our coffee. We figured he was concerned about us being in town, wanting in his business so early in the morning.

A short time later, before we were served, three colored men came into the restaurant, and sat down like they were going to eat there.

Back home, this would not have happened, we thought, as colored folks just didn't come in and sit in a restaurant where white folks ate.

A few minutes later, more colored people came in. By the time we got our food brought to our table, the whole place was full of colored people.

In fact, we were the only white people in the entire place! Thus, it dawned on us, that we had walked into a colored restaurant where colored people came to eat.

White folks never patronized a colored establishment back then, as colored people never entered a white restaurant. Not that they wouldn't have like to have done so.

My blood felt chilled to the bone. Not because I was afraid, but for the first time in my life, I experienced how they must have felt as a minority.

Consider and picture a time and place where there were separate rest rooms and separate waiting rooms for the black and white.

Try to imagine a time, when the rule that a Negro was to never enter the front door of a home, was so taken for granted, that when white people decided to leave their homes for a short time, they locked the back doors and left the front doors open.

Ordinary courtesies had no place between the two races. A white man thought nothing of sitting, while a colored woman stood.

In a sad conclusion, it has often been said that the major difference between Northern and Southern white attitudes toward blacks in past times has been, that in the North, black people were loved as a race and despised as individuals, while in the South, they were loved as individuals and despised as a race.

Permit me to share with you a true story from my own childhood, and how the years have opened my eyes on this issue of being prejudice against another race.

It is not a black and white issue, it's a matter of the heart

"Hey Leachabaughm, whatcha doing?"

"I'm picking out dem weeds for Miss Trulia, like she told me."

"Ya getting paid for it?"

"Yes, um, Isa paying me a whole fifty cents."

"Can I help ya?"

"If ya wanna, but I can't pay ya nothing."

"Maybe we can go up town and get us one of them soda pops, what do you say Leachabaughm Alexander Campbell?"

"I sure wishes I could, but my momma done told me I ain't allowed to go up there."

"Why can't you, Leachabaughm?"

"Because I'm black! Momma says dem white folk don't take a liking to us black kids coming in town."

"I'm white Leachabaughm."

"Yesum you is, but you different."

"I will always be your friend, Leachabaughm."

"I know ya will, that's good too!"

"I'll help you pick these weeds and then we will go play, ok Leachabaughm?"

"Yeah, sure, I'sa gonna always be your friend too."

So it was, during my childhood. Racial discrimination was predominate and abounded in almost every American city, even in the small one I lived in. In the eyes and hearts of adults, at least some or most, there resided a feeling of white supremacy, but as for Leachabaughm and me, we saw each other as two kids, about the same age and sex, who lived in the same neighborhood, and who needed a friend.

In reflecting on this time period of my life, which was more than four decades ago, I now realize my age had nothing to do with my color blindness. It was the influence I had received from my father. My father loved colored people, at least that was what we called them in my home, and colored people loved him. I, to this day, have not the slightest, as to how this came to be. He was raised on a farm, in an area to my knowledge all white.

I suspect he came to know and love these people, in the jobs he had after moving to the city.

Being raised on the farm, he most likely never encountered this race. Thus he either never had a chance to discover a difference, or there wasn't a difference, other than the color of their skin. I think the former part of that sentence was the case.

For now I have come to a place and point in my life, where I can look back and see things I never saw before. I am standing on a mountain top of life experiences, where once I was standing on the ground of trial and error. I have seen my heart travel from an attitude of indifference, to pride, to hate, to shame, and then to love, toward the Negro race. I am now aware of the deep emotional feelings, that were buried in the soul of my black brothers, or at least some of them.

I am also aware of how insensitive were the emotions and thoughts of my white brothers, and my heart and mind. This is the gap that exists between the black and white.

It's not the color of the skin, not the ability to excel or learn. In all things God gave both an equal amount of the same. The difference lies in the thoughts that have been fed and received and believed by both races.

56

Couples Grow Older and More Alike

Most recently as I meditated about being married to the same person for 30 years, something occurred to me which I find absolutely amazing. When two people live together this many years, their minds become one, even if they have both developed a serious memory loss. In fact, this is when it becomes the most important. I find examples of the following conversation almost a daily experience:

"Do you remember—you know, that person who came by? What was his name?"

"Yes, I remember him. Let's see. I think his name was—it begins with a B, I think it was. No, that wasn't it."

"Well, anyway, he was wearing that—you know, and we wondered if he was going to...and he did."

"I remember, but I think he already had and we were wondering if he was going to...or something."

"That's right. Man, what was that guy's name?"

Then later in the day, at the same moment, we both say, "I remember. His name was..." and we both shout out the name. Which is followed by "I think we should go out and celebrate by having a cup of...what we had the other night."

"So do I. What was that called? Was it—no, perhaps it was...."

Would you not agree that oneness of mind is a beautiful thing?

57

My Father's Love

I am amazed by my father's love. While yet in my mother's womb, I was the apple of his eye. And his eye was always upon me as I developed and grew as a child. When I reached that age where one thinks that they know more than their father, he lovingly let me find out how wrong I was, and he was there to pick up the pieces of my contrite heart. His love has met my every need which includes my mate of 30 years. He let me be the father of three children which has taught me even more about his love for me.

I have found the ingredients which are needed to be a good father are: kindness, mercy, patience, and strength. More important than these, however, is love. Yes, I am amazed by my heavenly father's love.

58

In the Land of Marshmallow Hearts

I want to talk about feelings. If you woke up breathing this morning, chances are, you have feelings. I would rather have a heart made out of a marshmallow, than a heart made out of stone. I want to be sensitive to other people's feelings, and in order to do so, my heart must be sensitive to my own feelings.

I find myself daily, around people who wear this heart of stone. They have no consideration of my feelings or other's feelings, and it seems nothing touches theirs. For us marshmallow hearts, this is a painful experience.

So often, I feel like a puppy, who is running up to his master, with his tail wagging with joy, and expressing his love. Then, only to be given a snarling look, along with a swift kick, leaving with his tail tucked between his legs, and head hanging down. Why?

I try to interact when I am in a crowd. I would actually rather listen than talk, but when I do offer a few words, it's like I'm the invisible man. Not only invisible but silent. When the conversation of the group continues it's as if I had not spoken. Feeling like a lost shadow, I become one. I want to assert myself, yet at times, it's as if I'm living in a world no one else really understands. A world where loving one another is more important than any issue. More important, than a held belief or disagreement. A world where being kind to one another, is the greatest thing a soul can do. Where are you, people of kindness, people of love? Where are you, God's children, born to be servants, and make love your greatest aim? How can such a spirit be so rare, on a planet where such spirits are to abide? Has "self" exalted itself so high, that there is no love left in the air for one to breathe or feel?

I want to talk about feelings. I want to be able to reach out and touch someone. Touch someone with love, without fear of having my hand bit off, or fear of being sued or rejected by a heart of stone.

There are so many to reach out to. The lonely, the broken, the lost. But even they are hard to reach. For so often their hearts have been hardened by a world full of humans, who didn't care, wasn't there, and wouldn't share. With just a stare, a person can say hurtful things to someone. Without a word being spoken, hearts are broken. "Why?" It's the hate and the pride, that has swelled up inside of humans everywhere!

I want to live, in the land of marshmallow hearts. Where all walk gently, speak softly, and express a sweetness in their life that takes away the bitter of all the wrong that is sometimes done.

I am not perfect! I am guilty! I have walked on feelings, and delivered hurt to others out of anger and pride. Only for short moments, however, as I knew I was wrong to do so. My heart told me I was wrong. Hearts of stone, have no voices or conscience that speaks to the one who wears them. Flexibility is required for a voice to speak, and a stone cannot be flexible, unless it's crushed and made soft. How does one turn a heart of stone into a marshmallow heart? It must be broken.

A marshmallow heart can be hurt, but not broken. It can be torn, chewed to pieces, thrown, dropped to the floor, and walked on, but never broken. Drop a marshmallow, and see if it breaks! It will bounce, it will roll with the punches, it will dissolve in the heat of love, or a cup of hot chocolate, but never can it be broken. For it is sustained with an ingredient that holds it together. In the human heart, God's love is always there to keep it from being consumed. Yes, you can consume a marshmallow, but not a marshmallow heart.

I want to talk about feelings. I want to love and be loved, but even those the nearest and most dearest, don't seem to realize this. If only they would drop their curtains of protection, the shields they have placed before them. Shields that blind them from seeing who I really am. Love comes with a price, and no greater price for love has been paid, than the price God paid for us. Can we not at least give a tenth of the love we have been shown by our creator, to one another. With this introduction being said, I now would like to share with you two stories, to help you become or to be able to recognize, a marshmallow heart person.

Love—What Life is All About

"We were made by his intelligence, and we are saved by his love."

I enjoy talking as much as anyone. I have discovered, however, being a good listener, is a rare quality to be found, and I learn more by being a good listener.

Recently, I was sitting in a large break room, listening to three very intelligent people. As I listened to their conversation, there was no question in my mind, that their IQ was much above average, and their educational background reflected this God given gift. The thing that troubled me deeply, was that they were exulting their intelligence, by belittling those who had less. One story after another was being brought forth, as each took a turn describing a situation, and mocking the stupidity of others, indicating that they were more intelligent than those they had belittled. Hearts of stone, walking on the hearts of others. Stepping on their feelings, without them even being there to defend themselves.

As I sat silently, my heart felt pain for these people, whom they had belittled. I wanted to speak up in their behalf, to defend them, due to their absence and ability to do so. Instead, I quickly raised myself from the chair I was sitting in, and left these intellects to glory in their wisdom.

To have power over the tongue, was my greatest defense. If I had started using it on these above the norm intellects, they would have declared me even less intelligent, than those they had belittled. As I tried to walk off my frustration, I pondered on how to make them see the error of their ways. How could I make them realize, that kindness and love, care and understanding, were much more important than all the intelligence the three of them had combined together? I concluded, however, that this was a task too big for me, and that to pray for these people would be the thing to do. Yes, even I had the ability to pray. We all do, and only God has the ability to change their hearts. He alone can take a heart of stone, and turn it into a marshmallow heart.

I thank God, I have been given at least an average intelligence, but I have never made fun of, or belittled anyone who appeared to have less intelligence than myself.

As my heart went out to those of us who are belittled by the intellects, I realized that it must go out even more to these intellects. For they lack the intelligence to know what life is really all about, "Love."

Little Things that You Do

"Why do you love me so?" "It's the little things that you do." Have you heard this before? Every person alive, has within them a desire to do great things, or at least one great thing before they die. Most of our life, is spent trying to achieve some great thing we want to do. We don't want to be a constant drop of water, we want to be a flood, and not just a flood, we want to be, "A Great Flood." Having this desire is natural and good. We must not overlook, however, the importance of the little things that we can do. For therein lies the path in having a marshmallow heart.

To list all the little things one can do, to make life a little sweeter for those around us, would require a book, not a column such as this. I will point out a few, however, to make my point on the importance of not overlooking something, we can give so freely. This is one of the great things about doing little things, they cost so little, if anything at all. To give of yourself, without expecting anything in return, other than to make someone's life a little brighter. It's the little things that you do, that makes a marshmallow heart.

A smile cost nothing, but says to someone, "I'm glad we met." To say, "Good morning," or "Have a good day," can turn the tide of events for one who receives it. A "Thank you," or a "I'm sorry," can mean so much, and only requires two words spoken in love. To say a "I love you," can strengthen a relationship more than silver or gold.

Have you thought of the little things you can do for others lately? This would be such a worthy effort to make. Make a list of all the little things you can do for others, and review your list each day. Not only will it change the lives of others, it will change your life. If your list, of little things you can do, grows longer than you have time to fulfill in a day, make a weekly or a monthly list. If your list is still too long, send it to me. Perhaps I will write that book.

"Why do I love you so?" It's the little things that you do. And besides, many of you have marshmallow hearts!

59

That Which Comes from the Heart

I have always loved going to the zoo. My favorite attraction is observing the apes behind the glass cages. I always denote a sense of sadness and guilt within my soul due to the expression on the apes' faces. When they look at me, I begin to discern emotions which they seem to be harboring that indicate a need for seclusion from the environment in which they are being exposed. Is it any wonder that they feel this way? They have been confined to a controlled area for humans to look at, laugh at and point fingers at. This makes the apes feel humiliated, embarrassed, ashamed and extremely self-conscious.

I made a short business trip to Chicago, which began with a flight out of the airport in St. Louis. As I walked to the gate, the announcement over the public address system expressing the airport's no-smoking policy was being branded on my mind. As I continued to walk, I discovered I was in front of one of those designated areas for smokers. What I observed with my eyes and perceived in my heart became a frightening revelation. The designated area was a glass cage with twice the number of people within its glass walls than it was designed to contain. The smokers were being confined for other humans to look at, laugh at and point fingers at. The nonsmokers passing by were doing all three, I assure you. As I spoke with the smokers inside, they voiced their feelings of humiliation, embarrassment, self-consciousness and shame.

The issue I am presenting is not a debate as to whether or not smoking is a hazard to one's health. What I would have you consider is a matter of the heart and, I believe, the beginning of a deep spiritual problem which has existed since Jesus spoke these words to his disciples: "Hear and understand. It's not what goes into the mouth defiles a man, but what comes out of the mouth, this defiles a man. Those things which proceed out of the mouth comes from the heart, and they defile a man. For out of the heart proceed evil thoughts, murders, adulteries, fornications, thefts, false witness, blasphemies." Jesus found it necessary to relate this to the disciples because they had not washed their hands and had been accused of transgressing the tradition of the elders. It was then, as it is now, they were teaching as doctrine the commandments of men. Someone recently wrote, "Smokers have not had their right to smoke taken away from them. They have had their right not to be embarrassed by it taken away."

I would ask you to think upon these things I have mentioned. Pray about it. Do an attitude check in your heart. And ask yourself what would Jesus do?

60

Only God is in Control

I do not profess to have an answer to all of the ills that plaque America. However, I do know the one who has the answer. Since the beginning of time he has brought nations of great power to their knees.

Like a flood, we are being told what our problems are as if we have lost all ability to discern these observations on our own. We are hearing from two political parties, two different points of view, with one message: You need us.

Children of God, take heed to what God is saying. He and he alone can promise all the above and perform it. In him put your trust. The words of men are empty and full of broken promises. "Fear not," says the Lord. He has not lost control, and he reigns in power to set rulers over nations and bring rulers over nations to their shame. Keep your eyes on the king of kings and cast a prayer before you cast a vote.

61

Tip Toe Through the Tulips

It was October 1996. For several weeks I had been hearing this voice in my head, encouraging me to buy some tulips and plant them for next year. Now I think tulips are beautiful. But I am not the "gardener type". I am not even the "yard type" of person. However, the voice persisted. Within days, I began receiving brochures in the mail advertising tulips. After giving them two whole minutes of thought, I threw them in the trash. After committing this act of aggression, I would hear the voice again telling me to plant tulips. With such persistence, I began to wonder if this voice was from God. Why would God want me to plant tulips? God knew I wasn't a "yard type" of guy. I don't like digging dirt, nor getting my hands dirty. I don't like pulling weeds or even mowing the yard. My wife is the "plant type" person. She loves plants! She has them all over the house, on the inside that is, and she has flowers planted all around the outside of the house as well. She loves working in the yard. Why doesn't the Lord tell her to plant some tulips?

Nevertheless, the voice became more persistent about me planting tulips. I received a sales catalog from a local store on a Wednesday advertising tulips, and so I decided the following Saturday, I would go there and buy those tulips, get them planted and that would be the end of it. My wife asked me what my plans were for Saturday, and I told her I wanted to plant some tulips. She thought it was a great idea. Are you surprised? Neither was I! So Saturday, at "High Noon", off we went to the store to get the tulips. We came home, quickly ate a light dinner, and headed for the yard. I asked my wife if we had a small hand spade to dig with. She informed me she did and then said, "I guess we should have bought you one at the store?" This would have been a good time for me to have bailed out of this job, but for some strange reason, I felt like I had to do this thing. I went out to the garage and found a rusty oversize pair of scissors, once used for cutting weeds, which I will call plowshares. "Where are we going to plant these tulips?" I asked my wife. I had asked her this question several times while we were eating lunch, and she just kept answering me with, "I will tell you when we get outside." I made several suggestions, but they were all bad ones it seemed. She informed me we would begin around the tire in our backyard, which she used for a flower bed. "You dig the holes, and will put them in," my wife said, like a foreman over a job. Silently and mentally, I said to God, "Who did you give this job to, her or me? She is just making me a common laborer." I took those plowshares and began to dig. I discovered before I could dig, I had to pull weeds out of the way. The ground was hard, very hard! I bent my plowshares just trying to penetrate the soil. When I did break ground, I found more weeds and rocks in the soil, which had to be pulled out, in order to have a place to plant the tulip bulb. I successfully dug four holes, and informed my wife I needed a break. I was totally exhausted. As I sat on the steps of our back porch, I thought of the parable of the sower, planting seeds on different kinds of soil. I was sure getting a first hand lesson of the rocky type of soil, and learning about the need of pulling out the weeds. After a quick cup of coffee, I headed back to work. I had bought a hundred bulbs, which I thought would turn our entire yard into a tulip garden. My wife had already used one bag of twenty, just around the tire in the back yard. Next, she told me to dig some holes where I had planted tulips once before, several years ago. They had stopped blooming, and the four feet of grass against the back of our house was looking a little bare. So I began digging holes once again. Where I was digging was more grass, weeds, and rocks than dirt, so my wife told me to go get the bag of top soil, and fill the holes back up. The bag was a 50 pounder, and I was worried about my back. As it turned out, something else got ruptured besides my back, and I don't want to even talk about that! We took care of this little section, and still had around 50 bulbs left. I noticed my wife was missing, after taking my third break within the hour.

I walked around the house, and saw this hug pile of flowers laying in the front yard. She spent a fortune on those flowers, probably $10—12, and now she was pulling them out like they were weeds, so she could plant tulips there. I refrained from saying anything, to her at least. I did make a few comments to God, under my breath. She wanted to plant 30 of the tulip bulbs around this small statue in front of the house, and the rest where she dug up the flowers. By now, all I wanted to do was be done with this job, which was making me feel pain in parts of my body I was unaware of until this moment. I dug a few holes, and made myself invisible for the next several minutes, so my wife could have the opportunity to do this job right. At last we were done, with the exception of filling two plastic garbage bags with the flowers she had pulled up. The instructions said to water them after planting, so I assisted my wife by holding a part of the hose, while she watered the area where we planted. She then swept up the loose dirt, and I held the bag open while she bent over and picked up the dirt with a dust pan. Now, my wife was as tired as I had become 10 minutes into this thing, and we decided we needed a nap. I thought perhaps, I would receive some special revelation in a dream as to why the Lord wanted me to do this thing. I didn't! So I figure that somewhere between now and next spring, some miracle is going to happen in relation to those tulips. So, if you should come by my house, and you see some recently dug holes, or some tulips striving to come through the ground, "Tiptoe Through The Tulips." Please!

62

As We Get Older Time Rages On

I wonder. Is it just me? Does anyone else sense that experiencing life has gone from a slow, dripping faucet to a raging river flood?

There are people living because they don't have time to die, and there are people dying because they don't have time to live.

It's as if someone has taken the remote control of life and pushed the fast-forward button.

I wonder. Is it just me? Have bad things just suddenly got out of hand? The traffic is bad. Customer service is bad. Crime is bad. Food is bad. Credit is bad. The delivery service is…oh, well.

Just remember the words or Shalom Aleichem: "No matter how bad things get, you got to go on living, even if it kills you."

As a final note, don't ask me who Shalom Aleichem is. Things are to bad right now I don't have time to find out.

63

It's Only Paper and Ink

It's only paper and ink.
What power can it hold?
How can it influence the mind of man
And market items sold?
It's only paper and ink.
What can it help or harm?
How can it change the day ahead
With the news it may inform?
It's only paper and ink.
Nevertheless I have no doubt
It's an item that has come into people's lives
They refuse to live without.
It's only paper and ink.
Why is it wanted so?
Perhaps it's freedom of speech
And our desire to know.

64

I'll Be There When the Last Teardrop Falls

I have found, that the ingredients that make a good story that is written from the heart involve emotions. Love, joy, laughter and tears. This is the stuff life is made of. There is a story behind every tear, if one will only search it out. This has been my greatest asset, in having a large inventory of stories to write.

Of that inventory, I share with you in this column three stories that were inspired by tears. Tears of sorrow, tears of wisdom, and tears of joy.

Poor Mary Don't You Weep

We were having a friendly chat, me and my new found friend, as I observed the treasures she had for sale in her shop. We shared something in common, her and I, our love for things from the past. Nevertheless, I perceived a feeling of sadness, hidden behind her beautiful smile.

As I was preparing to leave, I sat down in a most comfortable chair, which was positioned in front of her desk, in hope that a continuation of our conversation, would give her sorrow a chance to reveal itself, to a listening ear.

Within moments it suddenly surfaced, as she spoke of her mother's illness, and her concern for her father.

Her mother was dying, and she feared her father would lose his will to live, if he was left to live without her. As her tears began to surface, in an unrestrained manner, I found myself feeling the pain and sorrow which she was feeling.

The sadness in her soul, became the sorrow in my heart, and it was in this place of time that I came to realize, we had something in common besides our love for the past. We were kindred spirits in our ability to love, and in our willingness to share our emotions with someone having a similar heart, both sensitive and caring.

Her mother soon passed away, and with the passing of time, I thought of her father often. One day, more than a year later, I met my dear friend walking to work. I inquired of her father, and she informed me he had passed away almost a year to the day, after her mother had passed on.

As I finished my walk to work that day, I kept hearing an old song playing in my mind. Perhaps you remember it. The words went, "Poor Mary, don't you weep for me. The battle is just about over, poor Mary, don't you weep."

Losing one's parents, or for a spouse to lose someone they have shared their entire life with, is indeed a battle. However, my prayer that morning was, "Thank you Lord, for the poor Mary's that weep."

For when we lose our ability or desire to be sympathetic, towards the feelings of others, we have ceased to love. And when we have ceased to love, we have ceased to live.

Wisdom Mixed with Tears

I have always been intrigued by the words of wisdom, that often flow from the mouth of a child. Once I experienced this innocent phenomenon, where tears were a significant part of that occurrence.

A youngster asked his father, "What is in an apple?" The father thought for a while, and then replied, "Seeds, There are seeds in the apple." Then the small child asked, "What's in the seeds?" The father, looking bewildered and confused, replied, "I don't know!" "I know," said the child, "An apple tree." From the mouth of babes, wisdom shall flow like a river.

Once, a pastor was writing his sermon at home, for the following Sunday, and his son was observing him write it. "Father," he asked, "does God tell you what to say, when you write a sermon?" The father paused from writing and said, "Yes, my son, he does." The child then came up, and pulled on his father's shirt sleeve, and said, "Father, does God change his mind about what he says?"

The pastor, and father, looking at his son with pride, because of his interest, said, "No son, God never changes his mind about what he says to me." "Then father," the son said, looking rather confused, "Why do you keep erasing some of it out?"

A child, sees the world in a completely different perspective. They expect honesty, joy, and love to abound, without a selfish reason.

One must be careful in their presence, as to what you say and do. For wisdom comes from the mouth of babes.

The greatest proof I have ever seen, concerning wisdom from the mouth of babes, is a story about tears.

I remember when my son was around two years old. We were having family devotion time.

During these devotions, we each took a turn to pray, at the end of our bible study time. It was the first time we had asked my son to say a prayer. I said, "Ronald, it's your time to pray." After a period of silence, I looked at my son, and he was crying.

He was crying, because he feared that he would not be able to pray like his two sisters had done. Knowing that I was waiting, he bowed his head, and folded his little hands and said, "Dear Jesus, please wipe away the tears from my eyes. Amen."

Little did he realize, how much wisdom was in that prayer. It was an honest, sincere request. It was a promise our Lord had already made, to him, and everyone else.

These kinds of prayers always receive an answer. It was short, but to the point. It was wisdom mixed with tears, which can only be heard, from the mouth of babes.

No Time for Tears My Darling

For several weeks, a co-worker of mine has been in preparation making her daughter a wedding dress. Every evening she devoted her time an energy to this task. Thus, this became the theme of our conversation at work.

She spoke about picking out the pattern, worrying about the size, and finding the right colors and material.

Would it be done on time, was the question she lived with twenty four hours a day. Her daughter came home for a weekend visit, and she wanted to try on the dress from her mother had made.

Carefully, her mother assisted her in putting on the dress form, and then she sat silently waiting for her daughter's reaction, as her daughter walked to the mirror. Then she stood in front of the mirror, tears began streaming down her smiling face, as she said, "Oh mother, this is exactly what I wanted."

No other words could have said so much as these. The weeks of worry and days of stress, suddenly vanished with these words. Not only had she expressed her pleasure and satisfaction with the prospective dress, she had said, "Mom, I love you so much."

Now, with the weeks of preparation, going through catalogs, and buying items to make the dress form, far behind them, her mother was looking once again to the road ahead. As her daughter was trying to contain her tears of joy, someone heard my co-worker say to her daughter, "No time for tears my darling, we must get busy making this dress."

As long as there are tears, there will be heart stories to write about. And "I'll be there, when the last teardrop falls."

65

Is Your Best Friend Killing You?

During my last visit to see a dear friend, dying from cancer, his last words still ring clear. When I arrived at his home, he was looking off into space as if he was meditating, perhaps about the life he had lived and why it was coming to an abrupt end. I sat down beside him and started to light up a cigarette as he turned toward me and said, "You know, I used to think that a cigarette was my best friend, while all along it was killing me."

Is your best friend killing you? Is he there every morning to give you that burst of energy you need from a restless night, a night where he was deprived of your attention but never ceased to cry for it? Is he at work with you to comfort you in every stressful situation, situations you are convinced you can't handle without his assistance? In the beginning of your relationship he was content to be there whenever you felt you needed him. Now you find him demanding your attention and dedication. You give him this dedication and attention above everyone and everything you love. And your dedication to him is something to be seen. You stand in the cold and the rain to be with him, since you are no longer allowed to be with him in your workplace. You spend more time with him in your back yard than with the family who loves you and is concerned about his effect on you.

Is this thing you hold in your hand your best friend? Not really. If this has been your thinking, remember the last words of a real friend: "I thought he was my best friend, when all the time he was slowly killing me, feeding poison to my brain and creating illusions, deceiving me to no-good end."

66

The Things Your Kids Can Teach You

Being a father has been a learning experience. It has taught me the true meaning of joy and gladness. It has shown me the reality of sorrow and sadness. Being a father has taught me much about my relationship with my heavenly Father. Being a father is a learning experience, and your teacher is your kids.

They begin their teaching career the first day they are born. They teach you that you were once a baby, loved by parents, and you will never know how your parents felt until your kids come into the world and teach you that feeling of joy. Then they teach you how to hold the bottle right in their mouth, how to change their diapers on time, and how to keep them from crying, by picking them up on their demand. As they grow older, they increase your knowledge on managing time.

They teach you when to sleep and when not to sleep, how to prepare meals in the middle of the night and how to get your work done in a short amount of time, or not to worry about it at all. They teach you how to feed another person with a spoon, and how to have a great amount of patience in performing this chore. They teach you how to buy toys, clothes and give the best birthday party a kid can have. They teach you how to be a kid all over again, as you play with them, and they teach you their ways.

They teach you how to be in a thousand places at one time and how you could have been in ten times the activities you were in when you were a kid. They teach you to be a movie producer, a chauffeur and a business agent. They teach you to save so you can spend, and how to spend so you can save.

They teach you to be a doctor and a nurse, how to clean the bathtub, how to pick up clothes, when you can find them. As they enter their teen years, they teach you to be a psychiatrist, or go see one, how to worry yourself to death, or have faith in God you never thought possible.

The most difficult lesson of all is, they teach you how to part, and share some-one you have invested your entire life in. They teach you that all you have so proudly taught them, has been in vain, or so it seems for a while. Then comes the stage in your life, where they teach you that all your effort was well spent. They actually become mature, responsible adults who want to learn how to be a parent, like good old dad and mom, and they even boast they're going to do this job bet-ter than you did. And then they teach you the meaning of being humble, by admitting you did a better job of being a parent than they realized.

Yes, being a parent is a learning experience, because of the things your kids can teach you.

67

Old Man River

At last, I had arrived at the Holiday Inn, Texarkana, Texas. I had been driving for 10 hours, and was ready for a good nights rest. The night manager gave me a friendly smile.

"Good evening, need a room?" I pulled out my credit card. "Yes, I need one room, one night, two people." Saying it like it was an every evening event. "I think we can handle that," he said.

"Where are you traveling to?" "My wife and I are going to Dallas to see our grandson." I said, with a touch of excitement in my voice continuing the friendly conversation I asked, "Are you from around this area?" "No, I'm originally from Las Vegas, I landed here somehow."

"How about you, where are you from?" "I'm from Cape Girardeau, Missouri, home of Rush Limbaugh, perhaps you have heard of it?"

"I don't listen to Rush, but yes, I have heard of it." "You live close to the Mississippi River, don't you?" "Yes, I do, in fact the Mississippi is like our back door on the east side."

He handed me my room keys, and with an expression that seemed sincere he said, "I have wanted to see that river all my life, I really hope I get to someday."

Shocked by his statement, I responded, "You want to see the Mississippi River?" "I sure do." He said as he leaned on the counter to continue our conversation. "I have read about it in books, and I have seen pictures of it, but I would like to see it with my own eyes."

I couldn't believe what I was hearing. I had lived in this river city, that overlooks the Mississippi River, for 53 years. I seldom gave the river a thought, lest long to see it. As a child, spelling the word Mississippi seemed more important than the river itself.

Nevertheless, I do recall my mom speaking often about the river. When she was a child, she lived on the Illinois side of the river, just across from Cape Girardeau, and she enjoyed telling us about the ferry boats.

The Badge and The Helmet

My mom also spoke often, about being forced to move out of their home, because of a flood. They knew it would be coming in a matter of days, so her dad built a wooden raft they would be able to get on, which would take them safely to Cape Girardeau, where they could seek shelter.

The reason my mom told this story many times, was because of something my grandfather did that she could not understand, nor did I, each time I asked her to repeat the story.

My grandfather, who had been the first uniform police officer in the city of Cape Girardeau, took his helmet and his badge that he had once wore, and set it on a fence post, the day they left their home.

He left them behind, to be taken by the rushing muddy waters of the flood. My mom, as was I, was astonished that he would do such a thing. Did he not care about these precious items at all? He could have a least kept them for his grand-children to have had some day.

How many times I played and replayed this scene over and over in my mind. My grandfather, with his police helmet in one hand and his badge in the other, walking slowly up to a fence post, and sitting them on top of it, without any thoughts of how much they would have meant to someone like me.

As I was writing about this, reflecting on why he would do such a thing, I believe God in his loving kindness, gave me a revelation as to why my grandfather did what he did.

A Sacrificial Lesson

If the badge and helmet held no sentimental value, in my grandfather's heart, he would have discarded them long ago, before the coming of the flood. I believe they were his most treasured keepsakes.

Next to his wife and children, these were the things he valued the most. That is why, of all the things in the house, these are the only two items he removed. Setting them on top of a fence post, making a monument to a position he was once much proud of.

Then why did he leave them on that post to be surrendered to the flood you might ask? Inside the house, that was going to be consumed by the flooding waters of the raging Mississippi, were the children's favorite clothes, most liked toys, and items they no doubt treasured and held in high esteem.

Perhaps, my grandfather had noticed his children's sudden attention, to items they would leave behind. How would he ever tell them, the raft was only large enough to take them to safety, and all else would be left behind.

When they saw their dad set his helmet and badge, items minute in size, on that fence post, how could they plead to take their dolls and toys, which well exceeded the size of a badge.

I think my grandfather was making a statement, when he left his personal keepsakes on that fence post. A statement that said, "I will not ask you to do something I am not willing to do myself." It was an action that required a great sacrifice, thus an action which required, a great amount of love.

The Underground Slave Cave

There was one childhood story of mine I shared with my children, a myth about the cave, that ran from Cape Girardeau to the Illinois banks. A cave than ran beneath the Mississippi river, and about my quest to discover its location.

I was in the forth grade, and the story was being told, that during the civil war, slaves were transported to their freedom by means of bringing them to Missouri, and smuggling them to the state of Illinois.

Upon hearing this story, which I sincerely believed to be true, I went off in a search to find the caves entrance. I began my search at Happy Hallow, since it was close to the river and I played there after school. After many days of sticking my head in every hole in the ground, large enough to hold it, I decided the cave entrance must have been elsewhere.

I felt certain that the cave entrance had to be close to the river, for what would have been the purpose of doing a whole lot of digging for nothing. I then received word, that the entrance was in one of the older homes down by the river, probably concealed by a closet, or an outside shed.

As I observed the old homes that might harbor the cave entrance, I came to the realization of how difficult it would be for me, to have a chance to search these homes and find it. So for several months, I gave up on my search, content with believing that one of those old homes, was the house that used to send slaves to their freedom.

Then I received a hot tip on where the cave entrance was most likely to be. On Main Street, just north of Broadway, on top of what appeared to be a mountain a good spot for it without a doubt.

The rocks would indicate the probability of a cave existing within, and with the house sitting so high above the surrounding terrain, it would provide protection of being surprised, by unfriendly intruders. Which brought me to my next dilemma. How would I get to the house without being noticed?

I decided that they would never suspect anyone climbing those rock clefts, that stair stepped to their home, so one Saturday morning I started at the bottom and climbed until I reached the top.

When I reached the top, I observed of all things a swimming pool, surrounded by a black iron gate. At least that's what I thought it was.

Fascinated by what was before my eyes, I decided to take a closer look. When I reached the iron gate, I suddenly noticed two alligators sticking their heads out of that water, so I ran, or developed wings like a bird, and found myself at the foot of that cliff, within a record amount of time.

The alligators? They were evidently some kind of decoration for the pool, but in my willingness to believe anything is possible at that tender age, I was convinced they were alligators! This ended my search for the cave entrance.

Well, I did check out a report that there was a cave that ran under north Sprigg street, at Sprigg street and Olive, and sure enough, there was a two-room stone cave there.

For what purpose it was there, I'm still not certain. It may have been the cave entrance, however, I believe it would have been closer to the river than this. The house in which I now live is close to the river.

When the trains at midnight come down the tracks by the flood wall, they sound as if they are in my backyard. When my daughters were small, we were playing in the backyard one day, and found a large plank of wood, buried in the ground.

"What do you think it is daddy?" my daughters both asked. "Perhaps, it's the entrance to the underground slave cave," was my reply.

68

A Father's Thoughts About Love

If I were to ask my heavenly Father, "Lord, what would you want me to know above and beyond anything else," I am certain he would say, "I want you to know how very much I love you."

As a father of three children and one grandchild, this would be my answer to them. More than all the knowledge I have attained, more than all the wisdom I have accumulated, more than anything else I would want them to know how much I loved them. I believe the desire of most fathers would be for their children to know how deep and wide is the love they have for them. However, as I meditated on the importance of having expressed my love faithfully to my children, I sensed a deep feeling of failure in achieving this worthy goal. Yes, there were times when they observed my tremendous love for them, I'm sure. Nevertheless, there were times when they must have surely wondered if I loved them at all, such as tough-love times.

While beating myself up about this, I began asking myself why my children experienced these doubting moments of my love for them. As I asked why, I was gently reminded by the Holy Spirit of the times I doubted my heavenly Father's love for me, such as the times when I wanted to say yes and he said no. The times seemed endless when he seemed to be so far away in a distant land at a time when I needed to feel the nearness of his strength and support. Suddenly, by the power of the Holy Spirit, I felt assured that even in my darkest hour of despair, my heavenly Father was there with me saying, "I love you." As my children were in times like these, I had become so preoccupied with my need that I lost the awareness of his unfailing love.

This gave me comfort knowing that what my children experienced with me was no different than what I had experienced with my heavenly father. Even he had to use tough love at times.

I would offer one comment to conclude this lesson of love: Fathers, don't be afraid to use tough love when you must. Even more, do not fear saying to your children as often as you can, "More than anything else I want you to know how much I love you."

69

When in Shadow of Cross, Pray

As Easter draws near, our thoughts focus on the cross and upon our risen Savior. It's a time to rejoice and sing the chorus, "He's alive." Nevertheless, prior to this holy week the storms of life will continue to rage. Many will be experiencing sorrow and deep distress. For them, the Easter message will seem like those faraway places from a long time ago. I call this living in the shadow of the cross.

The Lord Jesus, just prior to his betrayal and arrest, was in the shadow of the cross. We read in the gospel of Matthew 26:36-39.

Then Jesus came with them to a place called Gethsemane, and said to the disciples, "Sit here while I go and pray over there." And he took with him Peter and the two sons of Zebedee, and he began to be sorrowful and deeply distressed. Then he said to them, "My soul is exceedingly sorrowful, even to death. Stay here and watch with me." He went a little farther and fell on his face and prayed, saying, "O, my Father, if it is possible, let this cup pass from me; nevertheless, not as I will, but as you will."

He said this prayer three times. Yes, Jesus was exceedingly sorrowful, even to death, thus feeling a need for strength and submission. Yet in his darkest hour, in the shadow of the cross, he went to his Father and prayed for God's will to be done.

70

Planes, Trains, and Automobiles Part I

Anyone who has lived for any length of time will agree, that there has been some drastic changes in the transportation system. As young as I am, I sit and wonder and marvel that the world has went from the 1947 Chevrolet, I owned at the tender age of sixteen, to sending space ships in orbit around this planet and to the moon. Over the past 40 years, I've had some real interesting vehicles of old, and I would like to share a few of them in this column.

Train to California

While working at Superior Electric on an assembly line, I discovered I had two weeks vacation time coming in July. I had never been out of the state of Missouri, and I had always wanted to see Hollywood, Disneyland, and the Golden Gate Bridge, along with Fisherman's Wharf, Alcatraz, and China Town.

To see all these places would require a trip to L.A. and San Francisco. Being only 21 and still single, I was able to save money for the trip, but working in a factory, I knew I would be unable to go first class.

I began planning my trip with the money I had saved. I could stay at the Y.M.C.A. for around seven dollars a night.

I intended to spend three nights in L.A. and three nights in San Francisco. I would need only a little amount of money for each of the places I wanted to see, thus, the largest expense would be the round trip fare to California. The most economical way for me to go was by train.

I don't recall the exact amount, it was somewhere around two hundred dollars. That is, if I was willing to spend three days going out and three days coming back, in one small seat with someone in a chair next to me.

I was told that I could take a scenic route by going north, through the mountains of Denver on the way out, and traveling South, across the desert of New Mexico. So this is the way I decided to travel. Actually, it really sounded like a great way to go.

Finally, the day arrived to travel by bus to St. Louis, and board the train at the depot. After boarding the train, I was assisted by a porter to my three-day seat, and advised that the dinner car was unavailable for this trip. I didn't bring a sack lunch for the next three days, so I asked the porter how I was suppose to eat.

He told me that there was a bar on the train that served Hero sandwiches and chips. I figured I could handle that, nevertheless, it was far from what I expected as my menu for the next three days. The next thing to happen, was my three-day companion came to take her seat.

After a long argument with the porter she reluctantly sat down and asked for his boss. Shortly, a man wearing a more important uniform came and asked her what the problem was.

She informed him she was a married woman, and that "no way" was she going to travel with a young man for the next three days. I felt both hurt and insulted, and I didn't like the situation any more than she did, but I decided to remain neutral in conversing about her feelings or mine, to her or anyone else.

She was told she had no choice if she intended to stay on the train, so for the next three days my companion sat beside me, without saying anything except for the words, "Excuse me," when she wanted to go to the rest room or the bar for something to eat.

I tried to accommodate her attitude and did fairly well, except I found my head laying on her shoulder the second morning I woke up. I didn't have a pillow and I guess my head was looking for one during the wild evening I had just spent.

The reason it was a wild evening, was the terrible dream I thought I had just experienced. I remembered seeing people running down the aisle in their pajamas. The ladies had hair looking wild and their faces unpainted.

The men had faces of fear as they pushed the women forward, and I can remember wondering if this was some kind of wild nightmare happening, due to the attitude of my companion seated next to me. That morning after removing my head off of her shoulder, I looked out the window and noticed the train was not moving. Since she was not speaking to me, I asked a person sitting across the aisle why the train was not moving. He replied, "Because we don't have a train."

I thought he was kidding, as the train had pulled over several times for cattle cars, who had the right of way when confronted with a passenger train, as we sat still for hours letting it pass us by.

"What do you mean we don't have a train?" I asked.

"Where were you last night, boy? Don't you remember the train catching on fire?" I would love to have had a picture of what my face looked like when he told me that. "Are you telling me the train caught on fire last night, and I slept through it!" I shouted with more than a little anxiety in my voice. "Sure did. They are sending another one to pick us up." Now it was becoming very clear to me why I thought I was seeing those horrible things in my dream. It wasn't a dream, it was really happening.

How would I explain this to my mom when I got home, was my next thought. She was worried about me making this trip in the first place. If she knew something like this could have happened, she would have probably pleaded for me to stay home for my vacation.

Well, I had 10 days to think about how I would explain the incident, but I intended to make the best of what was left of the trip and enjoy it. My first adventure on a train, however, was more than I expected it to ever be.

This article has become longer than I expected it to be. Over a thousand words already. Thus, I will make Trains, Planes and Automobiles at least a two-part article, with Planes and Automobiles soon to come. While on the subject of trains, I wish to say that I have always been fascinated by them.

My grandfather was a conductor on a Frisco train, and I have his railroad watch. The watch which he used to determine the proper time, to signal the train to move on down the rails.

And even now, I sit up at night and listen for the lonesome sounds of the whistle blow and the clattering of the huge wheels coming down the tracks by the river, which are only a breath away from my backyard.

71

Planes, Trains, and Automobiles
Part II

In part one I told of my first great adventure on a train, at the youthful age of 21. I was even younger than that when I had my first experience on a plane. I was around the age of 14, when one fears nothing and is willing to try most anything, well, almost!

HERE COMES THE PLANE, HERE COMES THE PLANE!

As a child, I really regretted not having the opportunity to be a Cub Scout. My cousin, Larry, took me to a few Boy Scout meetings he was the leader of, but I never got to wear one of those uniforms that make you look like you are in the military. As I entered into my teen years, I heard about an organization called, The Civil Air Patrol. I decided to attend one of their meetings, and find out what it was all about. I was impressed! They wore uniforms that looked just like the uniforms worn in the Air Force. They had some old rifles, disarmed, which they did maneuvers with. They had different ranks, and some of my friends were officers already. Yes, this was for me I would be part of the team and prepare for the United States Air Force.

The Major of this group was August Birk. Mr. Birk took a liking to me. He even gave me extra work during the summer, mowing his lawn and taking care of his yard. His wife would always fix me a sandwich after I worked awhile and noon approached. I never asked her to do that, nor expected her to be so kind. She was simply a precious lady.

One of the activities in the Civil Air Patrol was to take to the friendly skies in an airplane with Major Birk. The plane was a L4 I believe, and as I recall, an old World War II military plane. Major Birk would sit in the rear of the plane, and the student pilot would sit in front by the door. The plane could be controlled from both the front and the rear. This activity was scheduled on Saturdays, with all members having their turn if they wanted to go. They would keep track of their air time and log it in a book. I was a bit hesitant to take my turn, as I had never been off the ground unless I was holding on to a grape vine, however, I really wanted to go. When my trip time came up, I agreed to be at the airport Saturday morning. I met Major Birk and we walked to the plane. My knees were shaking just thinking about flying in that airplane. Nevertheless, I trusted Major Birk and his ability to keep me safe performing this event. I didn't trust many men or people as a child, but Major Birk was one of those people who just radiated a self confidence in everything he did. This made him a person who you wanted to trust.

He entered the plane, crawled into the back seat, and I climbed aboard and sat in the front. Major Birk closed the one and only door and started the engine. It made so much noise, that I could hardly hear what Major Birk was saying, but soon we were heading down the runway, and then I felt us leaving the ground. We climbed higher, and higher, and we were heading in an upward position, when suddenly the door flew open. The wind was blowing so hard, I could hardly take a breath. Major Birk shouted something to me, but there was so much noise I couldn't understand him. I turned my head around to make sure he hadn't aborted ship, and he was pointing to the door and signaling me to close it. "You want me to close the door" I shouted, and he nodded in a yes fashion. I was very nervous about trying to grab the door, as it seemed so far away, and the wind was pulling me already in that direction. I was of the opinion, that if I reached out for the door, there was a very good chance, in fact an excellent chance, that the wind would take my 70-pound body and send it sailing like a falling leaf. However, if Major Birk was to reach out for the door, he would no longer be able to control the plane, and would be sitting in the front with me. There wasn't enough room in the front for two, thus, I would need to bail out first. Either way, I was dead, so I reached out and grabbed the door. The pull was terrific, and I couldn't get it all the way closed. I did get it close enough for major Birk to grab the handle, and he closed it the rest of the way. Through this whole ordeal Major Birk remained as calm as if he was at home on the couch. I thought for sure I was going to die, right there on the spot. Well, not right there, but somewhere down below, close to the spot we were at in the air. We continued our journey, as Major Birk leveled us off at a nice peak for flying, and I began to relax. I felt like I was in Heaven. Previously, I thought I was going to get there before I was ready to go. Now, however, I was calm like Major Birk, and the melody "Off we go, into the wild blue yonder," came playing in my head. We had a wonderful flight, and Major Birk brought us in for a safe, soft landing, and I thanked the Lord we were on the ground once again.

I took several flights thereafter with Major Birk, and once I even got to go with him on a trip to Paducah in a twin engine airplane which was owned and piloted by Tom Myers as I recall. It sure flew different than that old L4, but the old L4 plane gave many a child the opportunity to fly the friendly skies for their first time. Later, I discovered that the larger commercial airplanes scared me even more than that little plane did. You could always land that small airplane in a field or a small clearing. You have heard the expression, "The bigger you are, the harder you fall." Well, this is true of airplanes! I have done it a second time, flapping my jaws until I have used over a thousand words telling you a story about one of the three forms of transportation, I have experienced in the past. This means, "you lucky person you," another article will tell of an experience I had in an automobile. It will be titled "Trains, Planes and Automobiles, Part Three." I would like to close this article by stating that I probably wasn't in as much danger as I have indicated in this article on that airplane ride with Major Birk. I am confident, that every child who went on a plane with that man was in the best of hands for such a journey. It just seemed scary at the time. I would also like to take this opportunity, to express my appreciation to the fine men who shared their time on the weekends, so the youth of this city, could experience an event such as flying the friendly skies, of Cape Girardeau.

72

Planes, Trains, and Automobiles Part III

Here we are at last! Part three of my experiences with three types of transportation most of us have used at one time or another. Part Three is about automobiles.

I was 15 years old and working as a car hop on Broadway at Phisters, a popular place in those days. I worked with another young man named Dennis. I liked Dennis, and we worked well together. Dennis was tall for his age, 16, and I was very short for my age. We looked like Mutt and Jeff, but we made a good team. Dennis was a very nice looking young man, dark eyes and hair. He looked like an Italian, and in fact, I think his mother may have been just that. I never really knew for sure. One thing I did know for sure, Dennis was very proud of his looks. He would stand in front of a mirror, for what seemed to be forever, and admire his facial features.

It was Friday night, and we were both working until midnight. Dennis, had just bought a car, a late forties model as I recall. It was a huge car, and he was very proud of it. He asked me if I would like a ride home in his new car, and I told him that would be great. When we got in his car, he asked me if I would like to go to the "Bloody Bucket." The "Bloody Bucket" was actually a night club on highway 61. I felt uncomfortable about us going there, and told him so. He informed me that we could get a beer there if we kept it under the table, and then we would go home. I went along with the idea because I liked Dennis so much, nevertheless, I felt nervous and guilty about what we were doing. We went there and had that one beer, at least that is all I had, and got back in the car to head for home. Instead of driving me home, I noticed Dennis was taking me on an old blacktop road heading north of the city. "Where are we going?" I asked him. "I want to show you how this car can run," he said. I looked over at the speedometer and noticed it was climbing at a rapid rate. "Slow this thing down Dennis, before you get us both killed." He gave me a daring look and shouted loudly, "You don't think this car can run fast do you?"

As he pushed the pedal all the way to the floor, suddenly, the steering wheel began to spin around like it was one of the tires on the car. Dennis began shouting, "Oh no, the tyrod broke, the tyrod broke!" The next thing I can remember, is Dennis shaking me viciously asking me if I was dead. As my eyes slowly opened, I noticed a hole in the windshield in front of me about the size of my upper body. I also observed a tree which stopped the car. I looked over at Dennis and told him I wasn't dead. It was at this point, I noticed the strange thing about his nose. It was no longer in the center of his face. It was under his left eye. "What happened to your nose?' Upon hearing this, Dennis quickly looked at the rear view mirror, which was no longer there except one small piece of glass. It was enough however, for Dennis to see his nose was not where it once was. He began moaning pitifully about his nose, at about the same time I noticed my head hurting. The pain caused me to lay my hands on my head, and when I did they felt wet. When I brought them down off of my head, they were covered with blood. "I cut my head, I may be bleeding to death," I cried, but Dennis was too concerned with his nose to really care. We crawled out of the car, and went to look for a house where we might find someone to help us get to a hospital. After a very long walk, we finally reached an area where there were homes, and we stopped at the first house we came to. Dennis knocked on the door. A lady answered the door, looking at a person with his nose under his eye, and the other with blood running down his face. "We need help, would you please help us?" "I am here alone," she said, "and I have small children in the house. Go next door and see if they can help you. We went next door, and the man who lived there agreed to take us to the hospital. We went to the emergency entrance, and they obtained information about us so they could inform our parents. Then, a doctor came up to us and said he would see me first. Dennis had a fit." "Doctor, look at my nose, don't you think you should see me first!" "Your nose will still be there when I get back," the doctor told him. "I need to get these cuts stitched up, before he bleeds more than he has," the doctor said while looking at my head. My thoughts were more about how mad my parents were going to be, than the cuts on my head. When my parents did arrive they were not mad at all to my surprise, they were just concerned about my injuries and happy that I was still alive. As I was leaving the hospital, I watched the doctor come to take Dennis back to look at his nose. Dennis was still mad that he didn't get treated first, and for some strange reason seemed to be blaming me for that. Things only became worse when his insurance company had to pay for my hospital bill, and it raised the premium he had to pay. This too, was my fault according to Dennis, and the friendship which I held so dear, departed as Dennis wouldn't even speak to me after that. I have since often wondered whatever happened to Dennis, and would love to run into him again someday.

Although this story ends with a note of sadness about a friendship I once had, there were some positive things that came out of that accident I was in. When I became 16, and bought my first car, I remembered that car accident Dennis and I had experienced. It made me a better driver than I might have been, if I had not had that warning about the danger that can occur when driving an automobile. I never had a single accident while driving as a teenager, and I can say in all honesty that Dennis is responsible for that. I can also tell anyone who thinks that I am a bit crazy, that my head once went through the windshield of a car, and that I have every right to be a bit crazy. Most of all, however, I have one more thing to thank the Lord for. "I thank you Lord, for saving my life, and giving me three children who have learned to drive an automobile!"

73

Life's Pace is Like a Tilt-A-Whirl

My wife and I enjoy waking up early so we can have some leisure time to go for a breakfast sandwich and coffee while reading the paper and discussing the events of the previous day. As my wife was taking me to work, I could not help notice the madness of the traffic and people as they were starting their day. Moms were driving their children to school with one hand on the wheel and the other holding their breakfast or applying makeup.

While observing the morning rush, my thoughts were overshadowed by a picture of a merry-go-round turning ever so slowly to the music of a beautiful waltz. I was mystified as to what this picture in my mind had to do with the business of the morning. My thoughts then turned to my school days as a child and how I had plenty of time to eat my bowl of hot cereal and toast and walk several blocks to school, stopping to observe whatever my mind took fancy to see. Yes, the pace was that of a merry-go-round turning to the rhythm of a waltz.

This led me to think of the days when our children went to school. To what could it be compared? Three children in different grades, sometimes in different schools and at different times, all insisting on rides to school in our car. Halfway there, one could always count on hearing, "Mom, I forgot something. We have to go back and get it." To what could this be compared? No doubt about it. This was the days of tilt-a-whirls.

This was years ago. I had to ask myself where are we now in this carnival of the morning. Once again, I became keenly aware of the happenings around us as we continued toward my workplace. How would I describe the pace which one travels today to get to work and the children to school? Most certainly it must be the roller-coaster ride of the day. Having a grandchild, it seemed only natural to wonder about the future and what the mornings might bring in his day. I quickly decided that the ride to compare it with has not been invented. It was shocking enough to go from a merry-go-round to a roller coaster all in one morning.

74

Miracle of Cross: Vivid Memory

As a child, the only air conditioning available on a hot and humid summer night were windows and doors. Thank God for screen doors. One evening as my mother stood at the screen door to enjoy the slight breeze, she suddenly shouted, "Ronnie, come here quick. There is a cross in the sky." I ran to the door, excited to see it. As I stood by my mom looking through the screen door, in the darkness above I observed a brilliant object in the shape of a cross. Mom took hold of my hand, and for several moments without one word spoken we enjoyed the miracle we were observing. My mother believed in miracles and taught me to believe in them as well.

"Let's go outside for a better look, Mom," I said as I opened the door. As we stood on the front porch looking toward the object we both observed as a cross, the only bright object in the evening sky was a full moon. We returned inside the house and once again looked through the screen door. And once again we witnessed our miracle of a vision of the cross. We both had a good laugh as to how we were both fooled by this illusion created by the screen door. Nevertheless, how great a moment it was as the two of us screened out every doubt and thought in our minds that we were witnessing a miracle, the miracle of the cross.

The miracle of the cross upon which our Savior paid the penalty for our sins is a miracle indeed. For had our Lord and Savior Jesus Christ failed to win victory over death and sin, we would be living in a world without forgiveness.

Victory was won, and we have a reason for much joy as we celebrate the victory of the cross.

75

Just For the Sport of It

I have found myself wondering why I never write about the subject of physical education. Could it be perhaps, because of the fact that I was shorter than a yard stick in junior high? If I was to write such an article, I could tell about how I was never asked to play baseball in the third grade.

Until, however, they discovered a pitcher couldn't find the strike zone due to my short stature, and they used me for walks, to get a player on first base. Or I could write about all the ribbons I won on play day in the potato sack race. All fun aside, there was that moment in my youth, when I exceeded all expectations, and excelled in the physical education program. It happened in my freshman year at Central High School.

One of my upper classmates, Ray O'Howell, wanted to befriend me for some reason. An unusual circumstance in those days, a junior acknowledging a freshman as a friend. Ray gave me a nickname which became familiar to many, he called me "Tiger." Ray was a football player, respected and admired by his friends and coaches. At first, I thought Ray was making fun of me by calling me Tiger. However, as he continued to call me by this name, he did so in such a manner, that I began to believe he meant it. In spite of the fact that I looked like "Charles Atlas," before Mr. Atlas ordered his book on developing strength.

We were informed one day in gym class, I believe by coach Allen, that everyone would be taking a physical fitness test. An annual event where the number of points one received on the test was recorded, and sent to Washington, D.C., at least that is the way I recall it. The test consisted of; set ups, push ups, pull ups, squad thrust, chin ups, and climbing the rope. As puny as I was, I had to live up to the nick name that Ray O'Howell had given me. He kept calling me "tiger," and I wanted to prove to my peers and coaches that he was right. There was a five minute time limit for each exercise, as another student with the coach watching, kept an honest score of the points we achieved. I went at it like a wild man. I remember doing fifty push ups in five minutes, two hundred and fifty squad thrusts, and climbing the rope twenty times. There were times I thought I was going to die, but I had a name to protect, a reputation to maintain, given to me by the big guy at Central High. I had to prove I was the "Central High Tiger!"

When all the points were counted, I had seven hundred and fifty points, the highest score earned, and a new record for Central High School in performing the physical fitness test. That week it was in the paper, "Ron Farrow, set a new record in the physical fitness test for Central High School, with seven hundred and fifty points." Boy was I proud!

The most amazing thing about this story has yet to be told. The thing that amazed me, was my father's response to this victory. It seemed to be his proudest moment. He insisted immediately to have the news announcement in the paper cut out, so he could carry it in his wallet, and show it to all of his friends. All through grade school and junior high I excelled in music, performed in every play and talent show, and he never attended once as I recall. I had writing accomplishments, with songs and poems, and not once did he act as excited as he did about this physical fitness test. He never seemed disappointed that I was not involved in sports throughout grade school. He once suggested I try to play basketball, and when I told him I was too short, he claimed he played on a team and did well. He never pushed the issue, however. He carried this news clipping in his wallet for the next twenty years that I am aware of, and perhaps even longer. In my heart, I must believe that my father had a secret desire to have a son who would fulfill a dream he was unable to achieve. A son who excelled in sports. Since my brother and I were both way short of being tall, or built for the game of football, my father may have gave up on that deep seated desire. When suddenly, something that came close, such as my setting that record on the fitness test happened, his joy is understandable. I am glad that he had at least that, to be proud of.

My three children were all born with my small built and artistic talents, and I was extremely pleased. In fact, I encouraged them to pursue their music and art abilities, and almost discouraged them to enter sports. One of the most frustrating time periods in my life happened, when my son played on a basketball team in grade school. To watch him sit on the bench, wanting to play so bad, and never given the chance to even make an effort, was a painful thing for me to bear. It was from this experience I wrote an article that expressed my feelings during that time period. Permit me to close this column with that article.

The Infinite Humiliation Award

With six seconds left in the game, leading by a comfortable margin, the tall basketball coach walks over to the bench. The bench where four young boys, seeking to be men, have sat throughout the entire game. "Ok, get out there and play," he says. The four young boys run out on the court, and play that six seconds with all the strength they have left after sitting out an almost entire game. They play that six seconds with all their might, with the hope that the following year they will be in the game and not on the bench.

Basketball: A game played by two teams of five men each, in which the object is to throw the ball through an elevated goal (basket) at the opponents end of an oblong court. A game! A contest entered into for amusement: A form of playful activity. Sounds like something that should be fun, for the player and the observer.

Discrimination against a persons height, color of skin, or economical status, should never, ever, enter in. Not uncommon, however, these four young boys, now in high school, sit on the bench in dismay. They observe the game being played, and the mistakes being made. They practiced on their backyard goals all summer long, now to be held hostage to the skills they obtained. Their hearts are on the court, while their hands and feet are on the bench. They long to make their parents proud, and their proud parents came to the game, but the four young men would prefer to be invisible, than to have their parents observe them on the bench and not in the game.

It's only a game! A contest entered into for amusement, a form of playful activity. Right?

Tell the young men who have the skill but lack the advantage, "It's only a game." Tell the parents whose hearts are broken, as they watch their child sit on the bench and not in the game, "It's only a game." No, they have been hurt enough. Tell the coach, who lets these young men sit on the bench, to look at these young athletics hearts, not their height, not the color of their skin, nor the size of their family's pocket book. Yes, look at their hearts and see if they are not winners. If playing the game is sitting on the bench, they are winners indeed. They should receive an award. The "infinite humiliation award." No one would deny they have earned it, but they deserve much more. Wouldn't it be a wonderful thing if the basketball games in the future, let those who make the team play the game? After all, it's only a game. A contest entered into for amusement, a form of playful activity.

Look what I have gone and done! I set out to write a column about sports, and ended up writing a heart article. Oh well, I wrote it "Just for the Sport of it!"

76

Give Hugs Today While You Can

Have you ever had an item which you treasured and held in high esteem? Perhaps it was a family heirloom or something your child once made in his first years of school. Then the day arrived where, because of circumstances or because your heart told you to, you gave that treasured gift to someone you loved.

Most likely in those last moments as you held it in your possession, a flood of memories filled your heart and mind—thoughts of how much it meant to the one who, out of love, gave it and possibly made it. And it was at this moment that you realized just how precious it was in all the years it filled your life with joy.

Each day we face this same possibility where the day will arrive and, because of circumstance, be it a wedding or a funeral, we will be required to surrender the loved ones we treasure, be it parents, grandparents, sons or daughters. And in those last moments as we hold them tightly, perhaps for the last time, our hearts will be filled with a flood of memories which will produce both tears and joy.

Wisdom seems to dictate, before that hour should arrive, that we should reach out to those around us and hold them tightly now and express the love in our hearts. Give someone a hug today.

77

Nation Must Now Make a Decision

We have this day set before us a decision and a choice of great consequence, a decision which may very well restore or remove (depending on our choice) the hand of God's blessing on this nation.

Before us is the choice to accept the immoral behavior of the president of the United States as tolerable and acceptable, or the choice to make known to those whom we have entrusted our office our desire to remove a president who has displayed and encouraged a lifestyle unacceptable in the eyes of our Lord.

The prophets of old predicted God's judgment on a nation when everything appears to be at its best—in the good times, not the bad. We must not be deceived by a flourishing economy. We must not fear the removal of president. What we should fear is the removal of God's blessing on this nation.

"Choose you this day whom ye will serve…As for me and my house, we will serve the Lord." Joshua 24:15.

78

All Sweet Mystery of Life

I'm in a reflective state of mind as I write this. I've been meditating on life, and what it is all about. Looking at where I have been, and wondering where I am going. Asking myself and God, not so much why, but what will come out of the fact, that I was once a visitor here on planet earth.

What Child is this?

I was born in 1943. This time period was good, prosperous years for most. As our country was rebounding and rebuilding from world war II. The late forties and early fifties presented a bright future with many opportunities for those who pursued them. A time for dreamers to see their dreams become a reality. As a child I was a dreamer. I pursued my dreams, and have seen many of them come to pass. Nevertheless, my years as a young child were anything but always joyful. I faced hardships and pain in which many of you would never imagine.

It would have been easy to have asked God why I had to suffer the things I did as a child. And as a child I must confess, I probably did ask God why am I living, and not what am I living for? Now that I'm no longer a child, I have an awareness of what has come out of my childhood experiences. An insight of this mystery of life which is so vast, a library could not contain the extent of it, were it written between the covers of hard bound books.

My childhood revealed a large part of this mystery of life, as it continued, in the years to follow.

I give to You and You Give to Me

As I entered my teen years, which is normally the bridge where one crosses from childhood to adult, I did so as one who had already became an adult very early in my childhood. This came out of necessity from being the child of an alcoholic father.

Thus, the years that are so trying for most, I was spared. Still, many of the joys of one's teen years, I was denied. As I sought to discern the mystery of life in my teens, much time was spent trying to find something to fill the huge void I was feeling in my life.

I fell in and out of love, with so many things, so many times, it became as easy as breathing. When I finally met someone who stood tall above all the others and all of the things I had tried, a person whom I knew I would love forever, she informed me on our last date she was engaged to be married to another.

Thus, the mystery of life continued. A few years of loneliness and withdrawal followed, and then I met my wife of thirty years. It was a blind date, her eyes met mine, and I knew that life for me was never to be the same.

Even this, however, seemed like a mystery I was yet to discover the answer to, somewhere over the next rainbow. For when one enters into a marriage, there will be storms to encounter, which are followed by the warmth of the sun, when the clouds of "self" are removed.

This also appeared to be a mystery, this lesson of giving, always giving of one-self. For what purpose is it? In God's design for mankind.

Reaching the Heart of Your Teen

One has not yet learned to give, until he has children. My wife and I have three. One of them left in the nest, and he is hanging over the edge of it, wanting to take wings and fly.

Talk about a mystery of life, children are the key to the greatest lesson one can have in solving this mystery of life. My wife is always saying, "When they're little they step on your toes, and when they grow up, they step on your heart."

There is no mountain of joy that stands as tall, nor valley of sorrow that lies so deep, as such as you can receive from your child. I cannot begin to imagine what life would be like, without children as a part of it.

For several weeks now, I have been attending a meeting on Monday nights, on the subject of "Reaching the heart of your teen." What a humbling experience it is to discover, after struggling your entire life raising children, you did it almost all wrong!

I did the best that I knew how, and even managed to do a few things right. My children seem to understand this, and have been more than forgiving about my failures as a parent. There is a bond between a father and his children that exist, regardless of the excellence of performance the father was able to achieve. This too, is also a mystery of life.

The Final Stretch

Like it or not, when one has surpassed the age of 50, they come to an awareness of how extremely minute the length of a life time is. Even though they take great joy in their grandchildren, and life is good, in the shadow of their heart they know that the day soon approaches when they will depart.

May heaven help and God give wisdom to the man who has not a clue to this mystery of life. For the clues have been obvious since their mother gave birth. There is a yearning in every heart for something that can only be seen and shared by all of God's creatures. And the fullness of this yearning can only be met by the one who created all things.

"Ah sweet mystery of life at last I found you, for it is love and love alone that rules forever."

Who Am I Writing For If Not For You

This is the month where our thoughts are on the things we are thankful for. Therefore, I would like to use this space to express my deep appreciation for the loyal readers of my column.

I wish I had the space to thank each of you personally. It has meant so much to me to have you come up to me at the mall or in a restaurant, to call me or write expressing your appreciation for my column. If you only knew how much this has meant.

Your kindness has been the fuel that has kept me writing this column month after month, at my computer night after night.

It has been the only reward I have received for writing this column, nevertheless, it has been the greatest reward I could ever ask for.

I consider each and every one of you very dear friends. I strive to make my column live up to your expectations. I sincerely hope that I have met that commitment.

Many have asked me to come out with a collection of my columns in the form of a book. If this is something you would enjoy having, I would love to hear from you concerning this matter. It is my prayer and my greatest wish, that each and every one of you, have a wonderful Thanksgiving!

79

Assessing Clinton's Behavior

I have been researching the chief characteristics of adult children of alcoholics, also known as ACAs, and comparing them with frequent questions which have been brought forth concerning Bill Clinton. The results have certainly given me an insight as to why he has acted the way he has. This is by no means an attempt to excuse him from his actions. Clearly, however, it indicates the need for one to get professional help if he is from a dysfunctional family or an ACA.

Question: Why didn't Clinton do the normal thing a person would do and confess his faults and ask for forgiveness?

Answer: ACAs guess at what normal is.

Question: Why is it that George Washington could tell nothing but the truth, while Clinton can tell nothing but a lie?

Answer: ACAs lie when it would be just as easy to tell the truth.

Question: Why did Clinton continue to be a womanizer after it was clear he had been exposed?

Answer: ACAs have difficulty having fun and with intimate relationships. ACAs are impulsive. They tend to lock themselves into a course of action without giving serious consideration to alternative behaviors or possible consequences. This impulsivity leads to confusion, self-loathing and loss of control over their environment.

Question: Why has Clinton associated himself with people of questionable character and remained loyal to them even in the face of adversity?

Answer: ACAs are extremely loyal, even when the loyalty is undeserved.

Question: How can a person have what it takes to reach the office of the presidency and then find himself in such a mess?

Answer: ACAs are super-responsible or super-irresponsible—or, for some such as Clinton, both.

Question: Why did Clinton get a dog and name it Buddy?

Answer: ACAs judge themselves without mercy. They are very hard on themselves. ACAs take themselves very seriously, even when others don't. ACAs constantly seek approval and affirmation. Only Buddy could meet these needs.

Question: Why has Clinton viewed Ken Starr as one who is pursuing an innocent victim with an unfair attack?

Answer: ACAs overreact to changes in which they have no control, and they feel they are different from other people.

Question: What are the prospects of Clinton hanging onto the presidency?

Answer: ACAs have difficulty following a project through from beginning to end.

80

Clear the Mind to Find Your Thoughts

One morning after my wife had dropped me off at work, I experienced a frustrating situation which became a valuable lesson in life.

I was the first to arrive at work that day, and I was searching for the keys to the building, which were in my pocket. I was having a difficult time finding them, because my pockets were full of wrapped peppermint candies. I had been at a restaurant the night before. Out of greed, I stuffed several handfuls of these candies in my pocket. Now they were keeping me from finding my keys.

After spending some time trying to find the keys, I had to empty my pockets completely of the candy in order to find them. Upon entering the building, I began to think about what had just taken place. I found no joy in not being able to find my keys. Why had I cluttered up my pockets with all that junk?

As I meditated about the occurrence, I thought about how sometimes my mind seemed to be full of clutter, almost to the point where a clear thought was as hard to find as those keys. The answer in finding the keys was to empty my pockets. Thus, when having a difficult time trying to think clearly, the obvious thing for one to do would be to empty the pockets in your mind. Empty out all of that junk that is up there. Throw it out. Lay it aside. Then reach back for the thing you are looking for.

What began as a frustration became a good lesson. So if you are experiencing frustrations in your life, empty your pockets and turn your frustrations into lessons learned. You will become a stronger person, and life will be taken in stride instead of strife.

81

A Street Named Good Hope

Forty seven years ago, there was a street in this city, that shaped my life as a child. It was one block from where I lived, when I wasn't living there, amongst my friends. A street where a seven-year-old child could safely go, and make five dollars a day shining shoes on its sidewalk. A prosperous busy street, used much for banking and shopping needs.

It was the only street in town, where you could have a hamburger delivered by a model train in a café, and see a movie for a dime. It was a happy place to be, a good street, a street that gave me hope. A street named Good Hope.

Put Another Nickel In

I have written about how I shined shoes on Good Hope street. Mostly in the taverns there, when I was only seven-years-old. I worked hard, I got my hands dirty with shoe polish, but I always had a pocket full of nickels and dimes to spend. Often, I spent those nickels and dimes at the Choo Choo Grill. I loved eating a hamburger there and watching that train deliver the food around the u-shaped counter. It was very entertaining.

However, I began to grow more fond of another fixture in the Choo Choo Grill, than the fondness I had for that train. It was a pin ball machine. It only cost a nickel a game and very often I would win four to five games when playing it. I loved the sound of that knock it made when it was racking up another free game on the score window.

One day, after shining shoes until almost evening, as it was beginning to get dark, I went to the Choo Choo Grill to play that pin ball machine. I laid a few nickels on the glass top and I began to play.

I was playing really well that day, and my nickels for future games were not even being used. I was totally engulfed in playing that machine when suddenly my father walked in.

He had never came up to Good Hope to find me before, as I was always home before dark. He was, to put it very lightly, extremely mad and upset. I grabbed my nickels and walked in front of him, as he marched me down the alley which went from Good Hope to our house on South Sprigg Street.

I was hurt, and I was confused as to why I was receiving such punishment for playing a pin ball machine. It was my money, I earned it, and if I wanted to put a part of it in that pin ball machine, I felt that I had that privilege.

I have recollected this painful experience many times over in past years. It was not until after I became a parent myself, waiting for my child to come home after dark, wondering why they were not home, and letting fear set in and take hold of me, that did I realize how my father must have felt that night.

It was then, and only then, that I knew why he felt it so important to impress on me, the seriousness of the situation and to never let it happen again. He got his point across. Never again did I stay on Good Hope street after dark, "to put another nickel in."

All in the Family

For me, as a child, the stores and the people who ran them on Good Hope street were my second family.

I am amazed now as I think about it, how accepted I was in this section of town. I was very small for a child of seven, very poor, and probably looked that way by the clothes I was wearing.

Just a small child covered with shoe shine polish, as I used my bared hands to apply the polish in those days.

Still, I made myself at home every where I went on Good Hope street. Places such as Unnerstall's Drug Store. Frank the owner was always so kind, as was his son, Sam.

I stopped in their place anytime I wanted, and the thought of me being in their way while they waited on customers never occurred to me back then.

Why? Because they never made me feel in the way, I was always welcomed.

I also spent many hours in the Club Tavern, watching people play pool. They had several tables, and many folks played pool there. I was there so often that they gave me a job racking pool balls for fifty cents an hour.

I figured if I was going to be there anyhow I might as well get paid for it.

Yes, the hardware store, the barber shop, the Bank, in fact every store on Good Hope street were like rooms in my "second home" away from home.

I was loved by these kind people, and I needed that love as a child, I think they knew that.

An Evening at Sam's Place

There was a barber shop on the south side of Good Hope street. It was in that barber shop that I received my inspiration to become a shoe shine boy.

I was not yet seven years old, and my father took me there to meet "Sam."

Sam, was an old, gray haired colored man, who ran a shoe shine parlor in the barber shop. He was always smiling and very upbeat in his attitude.

My father wanted me to see Sam's uncanny ability to make a shoe shine cloth (we actually called them rags back then) play music as he shined a pair of shoes.

Dad introduced me to Sam, as I crawled into one of the two big chairs which were joined together, and sat down for Sam to shine my shoes.

After applying the shoe polish, Sam got out that rag and began a sweeping motion on my shoes. As he did so, he began singing a song. As he sang, he started popping the rag by making a slack spot in it, and then swiftly pulling it out, until it made a popping sound. He was able to make musical notes with the popping sounds as he continued to sing his song.

Sam taught me how to pop that rag, and it became a part of my fame a few years later, when I walked the street of Good Hope shining shoes. However, I never achieved the same quality of skill that Sam had. I was offered, and I accepted a job in that very same barber shop where I met Sam a few years earlier.

I did not stay very long, however, as I wanted to get back out on the streets and find the business, rather than sit there and wait for it to come to me.

Nevertheless, it was indeed an honor to stand and shine shoes, where one of the greatest of them all had worked. It was still in my heart, "Sam's Place."

In Conclusion

There's a street in this city, where shootings occur, gang members meet, and I hear problems with drugs abound. A street the police should fear to tread, without a backup.

A street where many, if not most, refuse to travel or cross in the darkness of the night. Nevertheless, it has became a baby-sitter for children who live in houses without a home, children who have not been taught right from wrong. Children who see no future, experience no good, and sense no hope. A street named Good Hope.

For many of us Cape Girardeau residents, this area has great historical value, and holds memories we would like to see preserved. Our city is growing. As it stretches out from the river toward the west, the north and south borders must not be forgotten. If we can work together to save our downtown, we can work together to save places such as Good Hope Street. If our city wants a vision for the year 2000, let it be a city working together as a community reclaiming this part of our heritage which we have neglected for too long.

82

If We Don't Wait the Lord Will

Recently as I prayed for wisdom about a matter, the only answer I received from the Lord was wait. Wait for what? Wait upon the Lord was the reply. I searched the pages of my Bible like someone searching in the dictionary for the definition of a word. I kept getting the same answer: Wait upon the Lord. As I waited, I informed Him that we're living in times when people don't like to wait on anything. "You know how I am about waiting," I explained to God. "I don't even like waiting for my letters to appear in the newspaper. People will run over you at intersections when driving a car, because they don't want to wait." The Lord's answer remained the same: Wait.

As I waited, I started making what I considered to be really good suggestions to the Lord in prayer concerning the matter. "We could do this, or perhaps we could do that. How do you like this idea?" I felt that I had to be doing something. I couldn't just sit and wait. I had heard my pastor say, "Do what you can do, and the Lord will do what you can't do." I think what my pastor said was a very wise statement, and I agree with it. Surely God did not intend for me to just wait and pray. Nevertheless, that seemed to be the Lord's message loud and clear. After I accepted God's answer and felt content to just wait, the Lord began speaking to me about waiting upon him.

"Have you ever wondered why the most supernatural miracles in people's lives seem to happen in the very last tragic seconds?" God asked. "It is in these moments they have decided to release all of their own efforts and surrender to me. It is only then that I can do a work in them. Have you observed in the past when you were so worried and doing everything you could think of but nothing which would help, that handling it over to me was the only answer? It was the only answer from the beginning as well as the end."

Then the Lord spoke something to me I found rather profound. "If we don't wait, God will." If we refuse to hear his voice when God says to wait and pray and trust in him, if we try to take on the world and battle sin on our own or try to accomplish anything without the Lord, God will wait until we have exhausted every effort and have come to the realization that we can do nothing unless the Lord is the one doing it. Rejoice. He's alive.

83

Christmas is Celebration

Christmas is celebration, and celebration finds its origin in the heart. Down through the centuries, in times of love and war, has Christmas been declared since the ringing cry was first heard: "Fear not, for behold I bring you good tidings of great joy, which shall be to all people. For unto you is born this day in the city of David a Savior, which is Christ the Lord."

Christmas is celebration, with gift giving and feasting, decorations with scarlet ribbon, the sound of music and ornaments on a Christmas tree. Christmas is celebration, but these traditions that harvest so bountifully to surround the day have their significance only if they define the intention of the heart.

Christmas is celebration, but without the intention to express faith, hope, and love, which are gifts that cannot be bought and sold nor traded, one's gifts are bare, like a Christmas tree without ornaments and lights that no longer shine.

Christmas is celebration, and the attributes that exemplified the true meaning of the first Christmas are as present in this year of our Lord as they were the day the Christ child was born. Faith, hope and love, gifts without price, ornaments incapable of imitation, are found only in one's heart and are, therefore, unique.

May the joy and peace of our Lord be in the midst of your heart as you celebrate Christmas this year.

84

Get a Job

I have mentioned in previous articles, that I worked at the age of seven, shining shoes on Good Hope Street, and how I sold newspapers on Sundays.

Looking back, it seems I've always had at least one job, and sometimes two, in operation at the same time. Before I was old enough to drive a car, I remember working for Al Sanders, Colonial Restaurant, washing dishes. I made fifty cents an hour, working from four until midnight.

I can remember my dad sitting in his car, waiting for me when I got off from work. This must have been difficult for him, as he would have to be up at five in the morning to go to work himself. I never really thanked him for being there, but I wish I could now.

Another "Lesson Learned" I guess. Don't wait until your love ones have passed away, to thank them for the things they have done. I too would be getting up at five in the morning to go to my second job. I cleaned a bar on Broadway, called the Blue Note. This took around two hours, as I had to rotate the beer bottles in the cooler. Working eight hours at night, and two hours every morning, gave me little time for sleep.

I soon found myself trying to get some shut eye in my English class, which was right before lunch. My teacher tired of waking me up, and let me sleep through both.

Several pounds lighter, and taking English over in my next year of school, prompted me to be satisfied with just an evening job for a while. I was a car hop at Pfisters on west Broadway for a while, and I worked at Wimpys later, performing the same position.

When not working I was roller skating at the Mary Ann roller rink. I was winning so many free passes in their contest, they offered me a job. This kept me on the floor in skates, as a floor supervisor, picking up those less fortunate skaters still in the learning stage.

In my third year of high school, I enrolled in a new program where you could go to school a half a day, and work the other half. I made a grade for working.

I went to work at the Pizza King on Broadway, as a dish washer at first, but soon received a promotion to cook and cashier. Before long, I was running the whole thing, while my boss was playing pool at the Pla-More pool hall.

At the end of the summer, I was offered a job at the N'Orleans restaurant as a buss boy. Mr. B, the owner, spent a lot of time schooling me in how to serve the elite.

He enjoyed talking to me about the old building, and how he was once partners with Bing Crosby in an ice cream company. He had a picture of the both of them together to prove it.

Mr. B was stern with me at times, but he taught me how to dress, how to look, and how to act, to please those who expected such as this. After all this grooming, what did I do?

I went to work in a factory making toasters. I spent ten years there. Ten years on an assembly line making toasters is a long time, and would have been wasted years, had it not been for the friendships I made while working there. I still treasure those friends today, as I did back then.

In 1970, I decided to lift my sights a little higher, and put my personality to work for me by taking a job selling life insurance. I kept this job for five years, and it was good while I had it. One of the highlights of my life insurance career, was becoming a CLU (Certified Life Underwriter), and having an opportunity to write a five-part series article for the Bulletin Newspaper titled, "Why Have A Will?" I received a tremendous response.

The well seemed to run dry, as enthusiasm goes with a job, however, so I went to work selling candy, something people could see, feel and touch. My route was in southern Ill, and I had this job for ten years. It had its moments, especially when my children were small, and would ride along with me as my helpers in the summer time.

We really spent some quality time together, singing songs as we drove down the highway.

They also encouraged me often in trying harder, to sell the items that looked like winners in their large eyes. Suddenly, I was out of a job with this company, at an age where finding a job isn't an easy thing to do.

Not finding work, I decided I would become a hairdresser, and go to work with my wife in our beauty shop. I went to beauty school, and thought I was doing quite well.

When I was about half way through school, my wife informed me I should look else where for work. This was real encouraging!

I should have known my career as a hairdresser was going to be short lived, when my instructor kept telling me my real talents seemed to be in my ability to write about hair, instead of trying to do something with hair. I graduated, received my license from the state, and went searching at the mall for a job.

After several interviews, and on-site demonstrations of my talent, by ruining my mother in laws hair, I became discouraged and sought the Lord in prayer to help me out of the mess I was in.

While praying in the kitchen by the telephone, I received a call from a dear friend and member of my church. He was looking for someone to work for him analyzing asbestos fibers.

He would train me, and the pay was better than what I could make as a beauty operator, so I seized the opportunity, and I'm still on this job as I speak. A few years ago, before I decided to become serious about my writing career, I noticed I had a lot of free time on my hands in the evenings.

Time I spent walking over to the super market, to buy food items that would torture my body until morning time. Each time I went, I would become frustrated with the service I was getting, especially from the checkers. Thus came the following article about this job.

Stand Awhile in Their Shoes

Walking in the supermarket where I buy my groceries, I saw this sign, Wanted: Part Time Help. Why not? I thought. I have always wanted to be a checker, scanning groceries pass that beam of light, and have the price to magically appear on the computer screen.

Besides, they need someone like me. How many times have I stood in lines too long, while a checker, always my checker it seemed, was having problems of every kind?

For some odd reason, they couldn't get the money drawer open, or they had to bend over to fill in some kind of form, or count food stamps.

You would think, that after making me wait so long, they would at least smile at me and be friendly. By the time my groceries reached their destination of being scanned, the checkers would look at me as if they were going to throw the groceries at me, instead of checking them out.

I would always say to them, "Now take your time.", as if they had all day to wait on just me. I said this, not to be nice or mean. I just wanted to check the prices I was being charged.

So many times, their price was different than mine, and I often wondered why they couldn't seem to get it right. Yes, they needed a person like myself. I would become, "Super Checker Ron."

I applied for the job, and got it. Let me tell you about the person checking out your groceries in a large supermarket. They have most likely spent several hours in class at school, or eight hours at a full time job, before they ring their first sale at their check out station.

They stand on tired feet six to eight hours for less money than most people spend for Sunday dinner after church. They are barked at about prices being wrong, when the customer grabs the wrong item, (The one not on sale.).

The change in their pocket disappears, for little children who buy candy and fall pennies short, and adults who look them straight in the eye and say, "I don't have another five cents, and don't intend to pay it."

Their love for mankind, is diminished by hateful attitudes and lack of respect from the customer. They void off items constantly, which people have changed their mind about buying, after they have been scanned and inserted into a bag.

This locks up the checker's register, and they must wait for management to unlock it with a key, while long lines of people look at them with anger.

Stress becomes their companion, along with fatigue and despair. They are the first people encountered, after the customer has had to pay for the things they wanted, but felt resentful to have to pay for.

They must use time and caution in processing WIC coupons and food stamps, in spite of the long lines of people wondering, "Why is this taking so long?"

They do their jobs as best as they can, and sometimes do the jobs of others who don't. since the pay falls way short of the reward they deserve, a nice word from management would help.

But a compliment from management is as rare, as the bloody meat they scan and wipe up, before bagging it themselves most of the time. They try to work by the rules set forth by the store, but the rules depend on who is in charge of making them at the time.

So the next time you buy groceries in a supermarket, remember these things, and "Stand Awhile in Their Shoes."

85

Creator's Art

If I were to live a thousand years, I would still be amazed by the Creator's artistic ability which is beheld in autumn. Against the background of the deep blue sky, peppered with soft white cloud puffs being moved by the wind, a transformation gives new expression to the trees once so green.

Ever so slowly, yet constantly changing, the green-colored leaves become coated with shades of red and gold. Only the Creator knows how. At the height of their beauty and with the help of the wind, the colorful leaves are dispersed to be observed even more clearly by man and child alike.

For a while the fallen leaves provide protection for the soil and the insects. Thus it is only fitting that after such a spectacular event that cleanup time should occur. As with Christmas presents unwrapped, there is paper to gather. So are there leaves that must be raked.

86

Twas the Night After Christmas

"Twas the night after Christmas when all through the house
Every creature was stirring, yes, even a mouse,
The stockings once hung from the chimney with care
Lay now on the floor so empty and bare.
The children were bouncing off of the beds.
The sugar and caffeine had gone to their heads.
And Mama in her apron and I standing by
Washed and dried dishes which stood a mile high.
When out on the lawn there arose such a clatter,
I ran from the kitchen to see what was the matter.
I raised up the blinds with my nose on the door,
Thus cutting my lip, which today is still sore.
The moon on the grass still waiting for snow—
For this was the year of the big El Nino—
When what to my weary eyes did I see?
Nothing but a reflection of me.
When I was much younger, so lively and quick.
When I became, in a moment, good old St. Nick,
Swifter than eagles, when my children came,
Their presents were ready, and I remembered their name.
The day is now over, and my strength is far spent.
Like Christmas of past, I have not one red cent.
Still, I am much richer in memories I keep.
Merry Christmas to all. I'm now going to sleep.
Good night, and to all a good night.

87

Sunrise-Sunset. Swiftly Fly the Years

STOP; LOOK; LISTEN, to what I am about to say! Perhaps this month's column was written just for you. It is a subject which you are familiar with, and you will find yourself in agreement with the point that I make, but, perhaps you just haven't thought about it lately, or haven't done anything about it. If this is the case, "NOW," is the day, the hour, the second, to begin.

When I was around 10 years old, I used to buy candy in glass toys shaped like a train, and other objects a child could play with.

I quickly ate the candy, then tossed the glass toys in the trash. Why not? I could always buy another one by simply walking to the store, and plucking down another 25-cent piece.

If I had used up my earnings from shining shoes or selling papers, I could always dig up some more dirt under the front porch of our house with mom's tablespoon, and find those funny looking coins that were buried there.

The owner of the store never refused them, and I had my choice of any candy item on the counter for just one coin.

He never put these particular coins in his cash register, but instead, he had a little black bag he kept them in.

I reckoned it was because he couldn't spend them, or give them back to someone else in change. Years later, I discovered they were very old U.S. coins. Some may have been gold pieces.

Today, they would be worth a fortune. And those glass toys? If you could find one, it wouldn't be in a store filled with candy. Most likely, you would have to pay several hundred dollars to a collector to get one.

As a child in those days, the value of these things seemed so insignificant. As did this precious thing called time. In the eyes of a child, time appears as an ocean.

So deep and wide that there will always be enough. Then, after one has spent most of his ocean on frivolous living, they find it was not an ocean at all, only a small fountain, with a limited supply.

"Sunrise-Sunset" How swiftly fly the years. How precious is each hour which can never be retrieved? Time slips away, and one cannot put it in a bottle and save it for a rainy day.

Why is it, we don't appreciate something as important as this until we lose it? Now is the time, to use you time wisely. Make each moment count, for yourself and those you love.

Another thing we often take for granted, is our relationship with our spouse. The sunrise of our relationship, should still be there in the sunset years. This is not always the case. Why?

You Never Bring Me Flowers Anymore!

Try as hard as you can to remember your courting days. How much did you go out of your way to impress your mate? If you had treated your mate then, as you treat your spouse now, would you be together now?

Be honest in answering this question. Is it not true, that you have grown a little slack, in trying to keep your relationship as strong as it was when you once moved a mountain to obtain it.

When was the last time you said "I love you" to your spouse? Are your evenings spent embraced in each others arms, talking to each other, or sitting on separate sides of the room, with your minds and eyes glued to the television set?

Do you and your spouse still date? Do you still talk? Has the romance in your life swiftly flew away? Has your spouse said, "You never bring me flowers any more"?

If you are starting to feel I am preaching at you, please forgive me and know this one thing, I am preaching to myself. I need to be reminded ever so often, of the things needed to keep a relationship alive.

If you just happen to be able to relate to what I am saying, perhaps you need this also.

My wife and I have been married for thirty wonderful years. It hasn't always been a piece of cake, and yes we have both changed considerably since we met. Children do that to you!

Our physical appearance has changed, we look young, but not like we did when we met. We are both now wiser, which makes staying together, as important as it was, when we first got together.

Our energy level is not what it was, but many things that once demanded our energy, is not at the level that it once was.

We find ourselves very often going separate ways, doing the things we like best. (Her spending money, and me making it!) "Only kidding Honey, Really!"

The thing that has kept our relationship alive and well, is we still do things together. We still talk to each other. We still date, and still love each other.

And when she gets down and out, or mad at me, I still buy her flowers.

As we observe marriages failing at a rapid rate, and the hurt and pain that is felt by the real victims, the children, we realize how important it is not to take for granted what we have had for 30 years.

Like time, if one fails to realize its worth, romance has a way of slipping away. You cannot put it in a bottle and save it for a rainy day.

The relationship may change as it grows and finds strength, but remember, "Sunrise-Sunset, Swiftly Fly The Years."

Paper Roses—A Valentine Message

A song entered my heart today. One I have not thought about for some time. The words are "Paper roses, paper roses, oh how real these roses seem to be. But they're only, imitation, like your imitation love for me."

I have never gave much thought to the words of this song in the past, now, however, since my wife is working in a flower shop, the significance of giving flowers to someone has become more apparent.

The words in this song define the true purpose in giving someone flowers that are real. For when you are giving something that is real, you are being honest and sincere.

When the roses are real, they are full of life. Thus, you are giving and sharing life, with whom you give the roses to.

Yes, in time the flowers will wilt and their beauty shall fade away. Nevertheless, the thought, the act of kindness, that spawn this gift of love, shall never fade away. Giving someone flowers, real flowers, is a gift that says, your relationship is something beautiful, alive! And real. Not imitation, not paper in a heart-shaped box.

What kind of price can one place on a gift such as this! Money takes wings and flies away like an eagle, never to be seen again.

Love is stored in the heart and grows and grows, until it becomes a beautiful garden, wanting to be shared, like the beauty of a rose. May this be your best Valentine Day, ever!

88

Kangaroo Rat: Bureaucracy at Work

I would like to respond to a comment made by Dr. Kathleen Conway in a recent letter to the editor, which said, "Since species become endangered most frequently as a consequence of habitat loss, and since the two habitat types that we have most reduced are prairies and wetlands, it is not surprising to find that many of the species on the checklist of rare and endangered species are prairie and wetland inhabitants. We also know that the best way to protect species is to manage the environment in such a way that habitats are not destroyed and populations are not reduced to the point of endangerment."

Reading this immediately raised a red flag concerning an issue which I recently became aware of while reading the Federal Register. Here is what I read that really touched a sensitive nerve:

"From the Department of the Interior, emergency rule to list the San Bernardino kangaroo rat as endangered. The U.S. Fish and Wildlife Service exercises its emergency authority to determine the San Bernardino kangaroo rat to be an endangered species pursuant to the Endangered Species Act of 1973, amended." The summary continues, "This subspecies occurs primarily in alluvial scrub habitats with appropriate vegetative cover and substrate composition."

This is where it really gets interesting. "The historic range of San Bernardino kangaroo rat has been reduced by approximately 96 percent due to agricultural and urban development. All of the remaining populations of the San Bernardino kangaroo rat are threatened by habitat loss."

Does this sound familiar? When I read that passage in Conway's letter, I thought, she could just as well be talking about the San Bernardino kangaroo rat. After all, how would you feel if you had a hundred rats in your yard and lost 96 of them?

However, this is no ordinary rat. It is the only species of kangaroo rat with four toes on each of its hind feet. Currently, the San Bernardino kangaroo rat occupies approximately 3,247 acres of suitable habitat divided unequally among seven locations, which are widely separated from each other.

Factors which threaten the destruction, modification or curtailment of its habitat:

1. The expansion of human population. If we are to save the rat, we need to get the word out to those people who live in the San Bernardino Valley to stop having babies.

2. Construction of levees. We must stop trying to save cities from flooding by building levees and flooding the rats.

3. Sand-mining operations. If we want sand, we can go to Iraq.

4. A large pipeline project. Come on, folks. Which is most important a pipeline or a rat?

5. The closure of Norton Air Force Base for the proposed development of a site for the San Bernardino International Airport. The Air Force has been providing protection for these rats, and only God knows why.

89

Larry Niswonger Touched Our Lives

Someone said, "You have not lived if you have not touched the life of someone and left an impression that brought forth fruit." Such was the life of Larry Niswonger, who recently went on to be with the Lord.

I met Larry soon after buying my first guitar. We both shared a love for music and became good friends. Larry encouraged me very early in my musical efforts and gave me the opportunity to use the talent God had given me. Larry made possible my first trip to the Grand Ole Opry in Nashville. Larry and I enjoyed a performance by the great Patsy Cline at radio station WSM only to come home and read in the paper of her fatal accident following that performance. We learned that not even superstars are immortal.

Larry and I played music with many musicians in the 1960s and early 1970s, too many to mention. I am sure if they were still with us, and those who still are, they would say that Larry Niswonger touched their lives and that his music left an impression that has brought forth fruit.

In recent days, when Larry and I would cross paths, our conversation was always about the Lord coming soon. Larry was ready and looking forward to that great and glory-filled day, as am I.

90

Would You Like to Make a Wish Upon a Star?

Recently, two songs have been playing in my head and sort of getting intertwined. The two songs were, "Would You Like To Swing On A Star?" and "When You Wish Upon A Star."

In my head, the music I was hearing was to the tune of the first song mentioned, but the words being sung were, "Would you like to make a wish on a star?"

Perhaps you remember hearing these songs, "Would You Like To Swing On A Star?" was about being something other than what you are. The first two lines always amazed me, "Would you like swing on a star, carry moon beams home in a jar?"

I used to try to visualize someone being able to carry moon beams home in a jar. The thought still intrigues my imagination. It was a great song with a childish flair everyone seemed to enjoy.

With each changing verse it ended with, "Or perhaps you would rather be a…", then mention some crazy thing like a fish.

As strange as it may sound, there have been times I would have rather been a fish and some of the other things mentioned in the song than who I was. Being a human being isn't always easy. Being a child wasn't always easy.

In fact, I have had many to tell me I was never a child. Being the child of an alcoholic robs one of their childhood. I have been trying to find the child I never was by taking a trip to my past, then writing about what I recall.

Perhaps this is why these two songs were playing in my head. The song, "When You Wish Upon A Star," is a song with a positive message, but one I always found a bit unrealistic. The words say, "When you wish upon a star, makes no difference who you are, yours dreams come true."

As a child, I wished upon those stars many times and never had any of my dreams come true.

The thing that is important about me enjoying that song and its message as a child, is that I had wishes, I wanted to believe it did not matter who I was and believe that wishes really could come true.

I wanted to believe that, but I didn't. I had low self-esteem, another symptom of coming from a dysfunctional family. As a result, I lived in a world that existed only in my mind.

I lived in a world where you could swing on a star, carry moon beams home in a jar. This was far from being realistic also, but it was my shelter from the storm.

There were two wishes I recall as a child that I would like to share with you in this story. One came true, the other didn't. The thing that gives them common ground is they were both "painful" experiences.

How Much is That Chocolate in the Window?

I was around the age of seven. We lived in a house at 332 North Frederick Street. There is a post office at that location now. Between our house and Broadway was a small grocery store.

In that store's window was the most beautiful thing my eyes had ever laid hold of. It was a chocolate gun. It looked just like a small revolver, but it was made of solid chocolate.

I stood at that window many a time with my nose pushed against it for a better look, I do not remember the price, but I do recall it was more than mom could ever pay for such an item. To make matters worse, I began having a problem with a tooth. And, a solid chocolate piece of candy is not something a loving mom gives you when you need to see a dentist.

I had never had any dental work, which in those days consisted mostly of pulling a tooth.

Nevertheless, I had been to that office where one humbles himself in a dental chair and screams with pain for what seemed to be hours.

My father had, I reckon, some difficult teeth to pull. He must have also feared a dentist, as I do now, and for a good reason in those days, but not now.

Thus, I was the one who went with him to give him the courage not to turn around and head for home and share a little sympathy for him afterwards.

However, this made me extremely fearful of going there for myself. Mom knew how fearful I was about it, but I had reached a point where there was no other choice.

She asked me if there was anything that I really wanted. I told her of the solid chocolate gun in the store window. She informed me that, if I would promise not to cry, I could have that chocolate gun. I promised, and together we walked slowly past the store where the candy gun was and went to the dentist.

I cried, but my loving mother bought me that solid chocolate gun on our way home. It was something I wanted more than anything at the time. I got it not because I wished upon a star. I got it because I had a mom who understood me and cared.

They're Going to Put Me in the Movies

While living at the same address and at the age of seven, an opportunity came my way which many only dream about. I don't know how I came about receiving it, but I received a personal invitation to try for a part in a "juvenile movie" to be made in Cape Girardeau.

This is how Shirley Temple began her career, playing in juvenile movies. I was to see George Sanderson, Casting Director, on Wednesday, August 23, 1950 at the Broadway Theater.

My mom was so proud. And, it was for this reason I became excited about the chance to be a big movie star. I even began to believe it was my destiny. When the big day arrived, my dad took me for my interview.

Upon arriving, there was a long line of kids ahead of us. They were waiting for their interview, I suppose, as the age limit ranged from three to 14 and there were many parts to be cast.

After about an hour, my dad began to grow impatient. He was tired, no doubt, and he was really wanting to go get a drink. By then, the line behind us was as long as the line in front of us.

Still, dad had all he could take. He grabbed my little hand in his and pulled me out of the line. I say "pulled" because I recall not wanting to give up that spot. We left that day, never to return, and my chance to be a movie star was gone.

Some things are hard to forgive, and for me, this was one of the most difficult. I feel certain my dad failed to realize how important that event was for me. May you wish upon a star and have all of your dreams come true.

91

Prince or Pauper: Which is Which?

Within the past few days, the world has experienced the loss of two individuals, one of whom I knew and one of whom I only knew of. Society has defined the one I only knew of as a prince. Almost certainly, society would define the one of whom I knew as a pauper. This has caused me to meditate on the value which is placed on the rich and the famous and upon the poor by society's standards.

As I write, thoughts of the Lord Jesus come to mind, such as "the Prince of Peace" and "He became poor that we might become rich." How does one draw a parallel between the prince and the pauper? How can one define the terms of wealthy and poor?

Most any dictionary will define these words almost entirely as the abundance or lack of material possessions. Even with respect to material possessions, can one truly draw a parallel between a prince and a pauper? Most of us learn very early in life that one can be rich in material possessions and still be poor, just as one with nothing material to call his own can be considered rich in wisdom and love. Thus, should one conclude that a prince can be a pauper and a pauper can be a prince? Perhaps.

In the end, this truth has always been and will always be. The world will always focus its attention on material possessions and those who possess them. God has focused and always will focus his attention on the treasures of one's heart. Best of all, God loves both the prince and the pauper.

92

Good Hope Street: Time for Healing

It is time to stop the finger pointing and speculating about what the motives of Time magazine are and start praying for God to bring a healing to the situation that took place on Good Hope Street.

To fan the flames that already exist is perhaps more damaging than the very thing that started the fire. I have been a resident of this city for 57 years, my entire life. For most of the years mentioned I have lived within two blocks of Good Hope Street, both as a child and as an adult. Many residents who are my age or older have fond memories of this area of town and are saddened that it has become the subject of such concern.

Has anyone considered that the very God who created this universe resides in the hearts of many of the residents of the south side as well as the hearts of many others in Cape Girardeau? He resides in the hearts of city officials and those who enforce the law as well as all of his children, regardless of the color of their skin.

We are to forgive and to pray for one another, even those who have trespassed against us. Is it unreasonable to ask our city leaders and law enforcement to pray for those who feel they have been unfairly treated? Is it wrong to ask the residents on the south side to pray for those who have been placed to enforce the law and to be our city's leaders?

As we focus on prayer this week and ask the Lord to bring peace and a healing in this matter, we must be willing to surrender our personal feelings and pride and trust him.

93

Don't Let the Stars Get in Your Eyes

One of my main goals in life as a young teenager, was to someday be picking a guitar on the stage of the Grand Ole Opry. I loved country music, something I got honestly, I reckon, from my dad. I never had a real guitar until I was around 15, and it only had one string on it. I gave that one string a workout however, until I could save up enough money to buy one of those fancy electric guitars. I ordered it out of a catalog, and was so excited when it arrived. It was a nice looking guitar, but if I had an arrow, I could have used the neck of that guitar for a bow. I played on it any how and I must say it was great for developing finger strength and those calluses one needs on the tips of their fingers. I learned a few chords out of a book and was progressing fairly well, but I knew there was much more if someone would only show me how.

One day I took my guitar over to my friend Deeds' house to show off my stuff. Deeds was a singer and we got together ever so often to jam a little music together. While I was there, a young man about my age came by to see Deeds and he was carrying something wrapped in a blanket. His name was Louis Hobbs, and when I asked him what he had in that blanket, he gave me a proud look and said it was his momma. He took the blanket off and it was a solid body black electric guitar. It seemed everyone had electric guitars in those days, but I don't remember anyone having an amplifier. Louie sat down and started playing that guitar like he knew what he was doing, so I picked his brains while he picked that guitar trying to learn as much as I could. I did learn a lot from Louis that day and the days that followed. In fact, it wasn't long before Louie, Deeds, and I were playing music as a band in a bar downtown. One of the most requested songs that Louis did back then was his version of "Oh Them Golden Slippers."

After a few years of playing music with almost every musician in town, I began playing bass guitar. Playing lead guitar was where my heart was, but finding jobs playing bass was much easier and the pay was good, when you got paid that is. Deeds was wanting to make a recording in Memphis, and since I had never made a recording in a real studio, I looked forward to doing it. I agreed to play on his recording of "I Forgot To Remember To Forget." So, Louis, Deeds, Chuck, Bill, Paul and I went to Memphis, Tenn. This wasn't Nashville mind you, but I felt certain it was the path that would eventually take me there.

Chucks' lead guitar part and my bass part complemented each other extremely well on this recording. When two young men named Tom and Lee heard the record they solicited Chuck and I to do some recording with them. We made the tapes in Tom's basement, they were then sent to Nashville and became 45 records somehow, for those of you who know what 45 records were. I played a lot of music with Tom and Lee. I even joined them on the morning show which was on KFVS where they were regularly seen. They had a song titled "One Little Kiss Away" and were given the opportunity to make a recording of it at Lonzo and Oscars studio in Hendersonville Tenn.

They asked me to play bass guitar on the recording, and since I would be rubbing shoulders with Staff Decca recording artist, who regularly performed on the Grand Ole Opry, I thought I was just a breath away from fulfilling the dream of a life time. We arrived at the studio early in the morning and besides the three of us, there was a piano player who made records with artist such as Pete Drake, and Webb Pierce, and I could go on and on. There was also a drummer, also a Decca staff musician, and there was this guy who just dropped by the studio and asked if he could sit in on the recording session.

He played a Spanish guitar and his talent for playing it exceeded anything I had heard at this point in my music career. The piano player asked us to run through the song one time, and he went on to say that he had a shorthand system he had developed, where he would have it down pat and ready after hearing it only once. Sure enough, after we went through the song just once, he had it down to perfection, but evidently we didn't. He stopped in the middle of that song for the next eight hours, sometimes we didn't even make it to the middle. Every time he heard something that didn't sound right, he intentionally stopped playing.

We decided to take a break as we were all tired and the piano player asked if he could make a phone call. He wanted to call Pete Drake, and advise him that he wouldn't be able to play the piano part on the Grand Ole Opry that night for Pete's new hit "Forever." He played the piano on the recording and he said it was to difficult for most, to play it the way he recorded it. My mouth must have dropped when I heard him say he was going to pass up the chance to be there on stage, the Grand Ole Opry stage! I just had to ask him, so I did. "Are you telling me that you would rather stay here with us, making this recording, than to be on the stage of the Grand Ole Opry?" He looked at me trying to hold back the fullness of his laughter which he felt inside due to my ignorance and innocence. After gaining his composure he said, "I can be on the Grand Ole Opry any Saturday night I wish to play there, for a whole twenty-two dollars! I am making twice that much an hour doing this recording session."

Well, so much for getting the song right the first time! It then became obvious that once one obtains their goal, such as playing on the stage of the Opry, or any other goal they want to reach, the glamour and glitter of it is gone.

After being in that studio for 10 hours, Tom and Lee, and I headed the car toward Cape Girardeau. I fell asleep as my head found rest on Lee's shoulder, the three of us all sitting in the front seat, with Tom behind the wheel driving us home. Tom and Lee have both passed on and are probably singing together in glory land. Nevertheless, I think I can say for them and I, that the stars in the sky that night seemed to have more significance than all the stars in Nashville.

94

What We Need is a Passion for Balance

Often a word or term makes its appearance so frequently in the media and in our daily activities that one must wonder if there is a message being delivered which we should give heed to. The word that seems to keep coming into focus most recently is "passion." Statements such as a crime of passion, sins of passion and things birthed out of passion have become common in describing a person's actions.

I recently attended a meeting where the speaker gave a talk on passion with so much passion that I became passionate about passion. This led me to one of my favorite places of research: the dictionary.

Passion is defined as "an intense, extreme or overpowering emotion or feeling." If one would try to define the atmosphere and mood of the times we are living in, the words intense, extreme and overpowering would fit in nicely.

Emotions and feelings are running high—so high they are out of balance. Have you asked yourself or someone else recently what is happening to this world we are living in? How could something like this happen? Chances are you have asked this question within the past few days.

I would suggest the problem is we are living in a world which has lost the scale by which deeds and principles are weighed and destinies are determined. We have surrendered the power and authority to decide and determine. What we need is what we have lost: A passion for balance.

95

Tax-credit Editorial was Disappointing

I hope I can find the words to express my heartfelt disappointment in the view you expressed in your editorial, "Earned-income credit is new welfare attempt."

Perhaps it's because it is just days until Christmas, a time when the importance and the reason for giving are emphasized, that caused me to feel uneasy about the attitude you expressed. For whatever reason, my heart was stirred. The sarcastic remarks concerning the working poor and those who have found themselves at the mercy of welfare were not called for, but were cruel.

First of all, there is a vast difference in people on welfare and a family with two or more children and a household income of under $30,580. The working poor are those who earn enough money to be denied welfare but not enough to live on what they make. Those living on welfare can only live on what the government has decided they need to survive.

Your editorial gave the impression that to give was an insult. I was thunderstruck that you had the audacity to say, "It is time to lighten the burden on Missouri's most productive citizens," indicating that those on welfare and the working poor are not productive citizens.

I make far less than $30,000 a year, and I consider myself a very productive citizen. I was very productive for this very newspaper for five years, and I gave it all without expecting something in return. Nevertheless, who would say I was less than productive by offering my talent as a gift?

You stated that the earned-income tax credit proposal is a straightforward, no-bone-about-it scheme to redistribute wealth. With your "The rich should get richer" attitude, I say we need a Robin Hood to come out of the forest and to the aid of those who are being oppressed.

Have you read Proverbs lately? God speaks clearly about how one's attitude should be toward the poor. It is my prayer that your heart will be turned toward those who are in need as we draw closer to the birthday of the Lord Jesus our Savior.

96

Catch a Falling Star

As I was lying on the hood of my car, observing falling stars during a special evening for this event, suddenly, the following words of a familiar song were being sung in the sound room of my mind. "Catch a falling star, then put it in your pocket. Never let it fade away. Catch a falling star, then put it in your pocket. Save it for a rainy day." As I listened to the song being sung in my mind, the thought occurred to me, that these falling stars, once bright and brilliant, shining in the heavens, will never be seen again. I wondered with so many stars in the heavens, would they be missed by anyone, and during their lifetime, did they leave a lasting impression in the galaxy? Would the brilliance of their presence, and then the darkness of their lost, create a change in the heavenly bodies?

Unable to answer questions such as these, which were beyond my scientific knowledge, my thoughts turned to the stars on planet earth. Human stars, who once shined so bright. Stars that have brought courage and hope to our nation. Stars that have brought faith to the defeated, and stars who have entertained millions by their artistic and athletic abilities. Human stars, who have met the fate of death, or have fallen by the sword of disgrace. Once human stars, now fallen stars.

Like the stars I was observing falling from the darkness of the sky, I wondered what kind of an impact they made, these human stars, on those who once admired their shining brilliance.

Had they left a lasting impression, which would give birth to a life changing effect upon our planet? I can only give a brief, personal observation in answer to this question. Each and every one of us, would probably have different views and answers as to the effect it had on us, if any.

This is due to the fact that we are all individuals, with many personalities, different needs, and interests. Who was your shining star who no longer shines? What kind of effect did it have on you?

I remember when John F. Kennedy was elected president of the United States. Prior to his presidency, I really didn't care who was the president of the United States. His personality, and gift as a public speaker impressed me considerably. I felt his strength and trusted his judgment. I was impressed! I was 21 years old when word came to me that he had been murdered, by assassination. For me, and I believe for many, when this star died, so died a hope and vision. The entire country felt as they had lost a personal member of their family.

Anyone still living, can tell you what they were doing the day he was assassinated. His life, his death, left an impression, and had a lasting effect upon a great number of people. Perhaps John F. Kennedy was your shining star.

Or maybe it would be Martin Luther King, also assassinated. Was he your shining star? Did his flames of fire last long enough to make the difference needed in racial freedom? Or did he give birth to hope, leaving his vision "I have a dream" unfulfilled. An unfulfilled dream, that has gave birth to racial tension.

It may have been, if you're the younger generation, Kurt Cobain, lead singer for Nirvana. I have heard dozens of public testimonies from his fans, that his death and the way his life was taken, suicide, would have a lasting effect on their lives. I'm at a loss as to why, but I hope for whatever reason, the effect will be a good one. Did his star shine too bright, too soon? Was this what caused a sudden burn out? Did his death have an effect on you?

How about those stars still living? Stars that have fell by the sword of disgrace, such as Jimmy Swaggart, or Jim and Tammy Baker. Was your faith hindered, when their human failures and weaknesses were revealed? Did this have a lasting effect on TV ministry? How did these fallen stars effect your life? Or did they?

How about O.J. Simpson? A man who was facing judgment, as to if he killed his wife and her friend. How did the outcome effect you? Guilty or innocent, did it change your course of faith in sport heroes, faith in our legal system?

Now we have Bill Clinton, President of the United States. For many he has been a bright shining star. Has the allegations concerning a sex scandal made his star grow dim?

Just recently, we observed the loss of two bright shining stars, Princess Diana and Mother Teresa. Did you sense a covering of darkness upon the face of the earth after the sudden death of these two stars?

As my thoughts returned to the song, "Catch A Falling Star," I mediated on "How does one Catch a Falling Star?"

After a careful study of the words in this song, I came to my own, following conclusion:

To catch a falling star is to, "Capture the moment," to "seize the truth," to "perceive and apprehend what the experience and the lesson learned was all about."

To put it in your pocket is to, "Enclose the experience, the truth presented, and the lesson learned, in the region of your memory and your heart."

To never let it fade away is to "Keep the experience and lesson learned, fresh and brightly clear in your heart."

To save it for a rainy day is to, "Use or remember the experience, the lesson learned, in time of need, and when times get hard."

In summary, "Capture the moment—Enclose it in your heart—Keep it fresh and clear—For a future time in need."

In other words, "Catch a falling star, then put it in your pocket. Never let it fade away. Save it for a rainy day."

97

All We Can Do is Make the Best of Life

My first guitar was given to me, and it only had one string to play on. Nevertheless, I wanted to learn to play this instrument, and if one string was all I had to play on, I would use that one string to play a beautiful piece of music.

In life, we are faced with circumstances which we cannot change. We cannot change the past and the mistakes we have made. We cannot change the things over which we have no control. The only thing we can do is play the one string we have to play on, and that is our attitude. We have no control over, nor can we change, that which is inevitable. However, with the right attitude we can face the inevitable, and life can be like a beautiful piece of music.

Lord, teach us to have the right attitude about the things we cannot change.

98

A Different Kind of Menu for Last Meal

After reading "Last meals vary according to appetite" by Tome Harte, it appears what I once thought to be uncommon and bizarre is not all that uncommon. I still find it really bizarre.

For three years I have kept in my desk drawer an article I clipped from the July 31, 1996, Southeast Missourian. The Associated Press article was titled, "Convicted killer Nave slated for execution. Nave, 55, was paroled from the Missouri State Penitentiary in March 1983 after serving approximately 25 years of two life sentences. Eight months after he was released, Nave pumped 10 bullets into his Jefferson City landlady and abducted and sexually assaulted four hospital workers.

The reason I kept the article was a paragraph which described his last-meal request. For his last meal, Nave requested a 12-ounce T-bone steak, baked potato, onion rings, cottage cheese and fruit, coconut cream pie and a chocolate shake.

After reading this, I pondered how a 55-year-old man who has spent 25 years of his life in prison and who was about to be executed could even think about what he wanted for his last meal. How could this man, who knew he had only hours to live, have such an appetite?

Thanks to Harte and his article—which, by the way, I really enjoyed—I discovered condemned criminals who eat a "Harte" meal are actually quite common. Even some of our local celebrities were asked to consider what their last meals might be. Had I been asked, I would most likely have said, "A bowl of forgiveness and a plate of grace." And for dessert? "Eternal life in heaven would be good."

99

Hello, Is Anybody Home?

Are you living in a relationship of many years and feeling like you are living alone? Do you feel that you are being taken for granted? Are you asking, "Where has the romance wandered?"

I hope you can say absolutely not, to these questions. Nevertheless, if you are leaning toward answering yes to the questions at hand, you need not feel like a stranger.

You are part of a large group of people who have found their relationship has went two separate ways.

How it happens and what should be done about it, is presented here in a light-hearted way.

When a man first finds and meets the woman of his dreams, she is the center of his attention. She is all he can think about. He wants to see her every night, call her every day, and listen to every word that proceeds out of her mouth.

If she gets something in her eye, he will know about it.

He is the most observant individual she has ever met. He notices every new dress, pair of shoes, change of perfume, even the earrings that she wears.

Just be too tired to spend that extra effort on your hair, and he will tell you how he loves your new hair style.

He never misses a cue. He knows if you're feeling up, or if you're feeling down. If you say your mouth is dry, he will immediately try to solve the problem. Yes, you are the center of his attention. You are in the spotlight. You are the bone the dog has been trying to find all his life, to savor and enjoy. So you marry the guy.

And why shouldn't you? You never got that kind of attention from your sister or your brother.

The most familiar words you heard from mom were, "That's nice dear." And dad? He must have had a hearing problem, as he would always respond to your most exciting moments with, "What did you just say," and then continue doing whatever he was doing, in his own little world.

Your dog or cat would listen to you. They might even drool for you. But when you asked them for their opinion, about the most important decision in your life, they just sat there, looking at you as if you were confused, or had totally lost it.

Why shouldn't you marry the person, who is giving you the most attention you have received since you were a baby in your mother's arms?

You marry this gift from God, and treat him as if, he is God. You try to give him all the attention he has showed you. Sugar in the morning, sugar in the evening, sugar at supper time. You're always there for him.

You take on a job, or two jobs, to help him pay for his pleasures. You give him a son or a daughter, or some of each, so he can be a father, and be motivated to get out of bed, and go to work each day.

You take special pride in the meals you prepare, and the way you arrange the table for those special meals. You entertain his friends, whether you like them or not. You become Super Woman, when all of a sudden, you notice something has changed.

You had your hairdresser to cut your hair, giving you a totally new hair style, which made you look younger. And the man of your life asked you the next day, if you were still planning on going to the hair saloon for a hair cut.

You went out and bought the sexiest dress you could find, and had it on when he came home from work.

When he never made any comments, you went half way and said, "How do you like this dress?" His reply was, "I told you last Sunday, when you wore it to church, I thought it was nice." You have asked him, "Notice anything different?", so many times, he has a pat answer, "I give up, what is it".

When you want to go to bed early, he wants to stay up late. When you want to stay up late, he wants to go to bed early. When you want to read, he wants to watch television. When you want to watch television, he wants to read.

If you're in the bedroom, he wants to be in the living room. You go to the living room, and he wants to go to the work room. Finally, you get within ear range of him, and spend 30 minutes telling him all about your day.

Every once in a while you toss in a, "What do you think?" to see if he is listening. He is staring off into space, thinking only God knows what, and you scream, "HELLO, HELLO, IS ANYBODY HOME?"

Has any of this sounded familiar? I am of the firm belief and opinion that women, who are the most beautiful, sensitive and caring creatures God created, will relate to this article. That's why it was written from a woman's perspective.

Nevertheless, I realize that this situation may be felt and experienced by the male in the relationship. He may feel deserted, lonely, and disappointed, in the turns that have taken place in the relationship.

Perhaps both parties are feeling like the victim of the previous situation of turning separate ways. If this is the case, they need to be talking about it to each other. Adding years of the same, to a miserable relationship, for the lack of a few words spoken in love is absurd!

Most likely your life long mate will be open and sensitive to your needs, and their own needs. Renew your relationship, start courting again. You will discover a youthful feeling you have long forgotten.

"Families that pray together stay together." Couples that do things together will weather all the storms that come their way!

100

Learn to Let God Hold All of the Rocks

The other evening I went to bed early. I was feeling extremely worn out from the burdens that were weighing my poor body down.

After I went to bed, however, I was not able to sleep. The thought occurred to me that perhaps counting sheep would take my mind off my problems and help me go to sleep.

When I began my effort to picture sheep jumping a fence, to my amazement the picture on the screen of my mind was someone handing me a rock. The rock was the size of a golf ball, and I quickly tossed it out of sight.

After doing so, I was handed a rock the size of a basketball. Once again, I gave it a toss, and it tumbled down a hill out of view.

I was suddenly handed a rock that felt as if it weighed 100 pounds, and it was as wide as my two arms could reach out to hold it. At first, my legs began to tremble from weakness, which was followed by a quick drop to my knees. The rock was still before me with all of its weight resting on the palm of my hands.

Out of desperation, I cried out to the Lord: "Please, Lord, take this rock from me and give me rest."

I saw another hand reaching out, and it took the rock away. I knew it was the hand of the Lord. He wants us to hand him our problems and the burdens that weigh us down. He was showing me that until we are willing to trust and hand him life's little rocks, we will only be faced with much larger rocks to handle.

Looking back over the past few weeks, I wish now I had handed him that golf ball-sized rock.

101

Jesus' Promises Give Comfort When News is Bad

Remember the song, "Don't Worry, Be Happy"? A lot of folks are having a hard time singing this song in recent days. With the bad news from Wall Street and the rising cost of health care, many are at their wit's end. I hear the fears being expressed almost daily.

This tells me some people have built their house on the wrong foundation. Jesus says all those who come and listen and obey him are like a man who builds a house on a strong foundation laid upon the underlying rock.

In Luke, chapter 5, Jesus says, "What happiness is there for you who are poor, for the kingdom of God is yours! What happiness there is for you who are now hungry, for you are going to be satisfied! What happiness there is for you who weep, for the time will come when you will laugh with joy! What happiness it is when others hate you and exclude you and insult you and smear your name because you are mine! When that happens, rejoice! For you will have a great reward awaiting you in heaven."

Jesus said don't worry, be happy. May I encourage you to grab hold of what you have just read. Take it to heart. It will lift you out of the darkness and into the light.

102

Born Free—To Follow Your Heart

One of my favorite movies of all times is titled "Born Free." This is also the title of a song from the movie, which is a favorite song of mine as well. I believe the reason I find the song and movie so appealing is the theme of them both. The theme is to be born with the freedom to follow your heart. For me, this means to live your life for the purpose you were created. The problem begins when outside forces try to change that purpose.

Caught in a Trap

A coyote is most likely not your favorite animal. Actually, it is not an animal I would bring home and ask my wife if I could keep it for a pet. However, I worked with a man who was a trapper and this was one of his favorite things to go after. As a lover of all of God's creatures and a defender for their right to live, I wrote a story for my friend to read, hoping to change his mind about pursuing them. It didn't even touch his big toe less touch his heart, but it points out my desire and deep conviction that one born free should be able to follow their heart without outside forces interfering for their own personal gain.

NOTE: If you are a trapper, be an open-minded trapper and bear with me as you read this. We all have a right to our opinion, whatever it might be.

On a journey of a familiar path, the coyote suddenly found himself trapped by the tightfitting metal surrounding his leg. Born free to pursue his life in the wilderness, he now found himself caught in a trap. A victim of a harmful hostile influence. With his end still uncertain, he was forced to lay helplessly and await his fate. In the still of the night as he laid there, one must wonder what may have crossed his mind. Perhaps he thought of the other coyotes, with whom he ran with on a daily journey, had they questioned what had happened to him? Or, perhaps he wondered if he would ever see them again? He may have been asking himself why he had lived such a life of freedom, only to now be bound by a metal clamp. A trap place there by a foe, which took him without warning, nor offered him the challenge of a fight for survival.

As the sunlight of the morning penetrated the shade of the trees, the coyote's ears perked slightly upward to the sound of the heavy footsteps of the predator coming after his prey. As the coyotes eyes came into contact with the human, who must have appeared as a giant in comparison with his small frame, he displayed his anger and anguish of the abuse inflicted upon him by showing his sharp white teeth. The human, his predator, showed no fear, as the predator and the prey were not on common ground.

The coyote, caught in a trap, could not defend himself against the bright metal barrel of the gun, which was aimed in a position directly between his eyes. Before the sound of the gun shot echoed through the forest, the life of the coyote came to an end. Not to become food, nor because he had attacked his predator or came near his home. His life of freedom to follow his heart came to an end so his outer garment could be removed and sold. To be sold for money. Not for the trappers survival, but for money to be spent on things the trapper could have lived without. I wonder, do you? Who is it really that is caught in a trap? The coyote or the trapper?

In a time period where synthetic fibers are being developed at a rapid pace, the need to interfere with the freedom of animals living in the wilderness is simply not justified for the purpose of obtaining a fur that can be sold!

While the above story is fiction, it is a subject of much concern. On a more lighter side, permit me to share with you a true story about a friend of mine. It is a perfect story for someone who was born free to follow his heart. However, there were some who thought differently about his destiny. This friend was a dog, and his name was "Big Boy."

Big Boy, Peanut Butter Crackers and Me

I was sitting on the front porch steps of our house when I first met him. I played outside often in the summer, mostly by myself, using my imagination to its fullest. I had just opened a package of peanut butter crackers, which I bought from the tall green candy machine in Mr. Maier's service station. The station was next to our house on the south side and there was a cleaner on the north side. This is where he lived, my new found friend, Big Boy. He came running up the sidewalk

I had so often sped down with my shiny red scooter and just about as fast. He sat down beside me and the first thing I noticed was his large brown eyes.

They looked so sad, and I seem to recall tears flowing from those eyes which just stole my heart away. He would look at me, and then look at my peanut cracker, then once again look back at me. Two things were very evident.

First, that he was very hungry, and secondly was that he wanted one of my peanut butter crackers!

I felt we should be properly introduced before I started sharing my food with him so I told him my name and gave him one. I named him Big Boy.

He was white with brown spots and long hair, and appeared at least to me, to be a big dog, and a boy dog. Thus, Big Boy seemed to be a proper name.

He continued to look at me with those big brown eyes that were looking deep into mind and kept asking, "Can I have a peanut butter cracker?" The package contained six crackers, so I gave Big Boy two and I ate four. He swallowed his with one bite! We became the best of friends, and he would come to see me every day. He loved to run, and enjoyed bringing me sticks for him to fetch.

Every day that summer we found ourselves enjoying our peanut butter crackers, and playing to our utmost ability. It was easy to see that Big Boy wanted to be a young boy's best friend. Here was a dog that was following his heart. After a week or two I started giving Big Boy three crackers and I would eat the other three as a treat. Soon, it became four for Big Boy and two for me. Eventually, Big Boy was getting all six of the crackers and I had none. I did not regret him having them, however, as he was my daily companion and he brought me lots of joy.

Then came the day I did not see Big Boy anywhere around. He always came to get his morning peanut butter crackers and I was afraid something had happened to him when he did not show up. I quickly ran over to the cleaning business where he lived to find out what had happened. One of the owners came to the door and asked me how she might help me.

"What became of your dog?" I asked with a voice of much concern. She told me they had given him to some friends who lived on a farm. "Why?" I asked with tears in my eyes. She told me Big Boy was a hunting dog, a bird dog, and once a very good one. Then suddenly, he had quit spotting and retrieving the birds like he used to. They had tried everything they knew to get him to make a comeback, the main thing being not feeding him for days so he would be hungry and perform better. For some strange reason it just didn't work.

Immediately, even as she spoke, a picture of six peanut butter crackers appeared in my mind. Then a picture of Big Boy eating them day after day. I felt like I had done something really bad. It was all my fault, if only I had not gave him those peanut butter crackers. I went home feeling so sad, I was missing my friend.

Looking back, now many years later, I have no regret I gave Big Boy those peanut butter crackers. He may have been a bird dog to those people at the cleaners, but to me he was a friend. A friend who was following his heart. A friend who came to spend the summer to play and enjoy those peanut butter crackers. It was a summer where in my little world there was only Big Boy, peanut butter crackers and me. Just the two of us, born free to follow our heart!

103

Author Provided Many Kind Words of Encouragement

I received a letter April 22 from the family of Marjorie Holmes—a letter I knew would come one day as an unwelcome visitor. Just beneath her photograph was written, "It is with sadness that we announce the passing of our beloved mother."

Marjorie Holmes loved life, people and her profession as a writer of best-selling books and articles from the heart. It was her book, "Writing Articles from the Heart," that inspired my column, "Written from the Heart," which appeared in this newspaper for five years.

Holmes supported and guided me with her words of encouragement. She gave of her time by reading everything I sent her and the writings I had published. I, along with others throughout the world who have been touched by her love and kindness, will miss her so much.

She wrote me the following once in a letter: "We may never meet face to face in this life. Nevertheless, we will most certainly meet in the life to come."

104

How Much Sacrifice is Really Needed

Recently, my grandson, Elijah, found a turtle. He wanted to keep it as a pet. I told him the turtle should be set free, but his Nana told him he could keep the turtle if he kept it in a box in our backyard. I protested by saying the turtle would die of hunger, but Elijah insisted he would make sure the turtle had something to eat.

Elijah loves bugs. He will go to any length to protect them. His favorite bugs are "ball bugs." At least that is what I called them as a child. Elijah calls them rolly-pollies. We gave the turtle tomatoes and other vegetables to eat. However, the turtle was not into vegetarianism. The turtle refused to eat. The only thing my grandson observed that the turtle would eat were ball bugs. For the next several days, Elijah reluctantly would find a few ball bugs and put them in the turtle's box. I could see the pain on Elijah's face.

One end of the turtle's box began to collapse from pulling on it. I warned Elijah that the turtle would get out of the box if it wasn't replaced. Elijah didn't seem alarmed that the turtle might find its freedom. I sense that he almost welcomed the idea. He had come face to face with an all-important question: How many ball bugs do you sacrifice to save a turtle?

In the national news, Ehud Barak, the Israeli prime minister, and Palestinian leader Yasir Arafat are asking the same question.

As we prepare to elect a new leader for our country, let us reflect on the past eight years. What price have we paid in terms of concession and sacrifice? Have we lost values that were once dear to our heart? How many ball bugs do we sacrifice to save a turtle?

105

Everybody's, Somebody's Fool

"Everybody's somebody's fool. Everybody's somebody's baby, there are no exceptions to the rule, everybody's somebody's fool."

When I was in junior high school, I lived on north Middle Street, in the Red Star District. I caught the school bus at the fire station along with several others who lived in that part of town. I always sat by myself on that bus by choice, as I was kind of a loner.

Not that I wanted to be, mind you, I just didn't trust people much. One morning as I stepped on the bus, a beautiful blonde whom I had a crush on asked me to sit with her on the bus. I was shocked by her invitation, but quite excited for the opportunity. So I sat down beside her, and as the bus left the fire station she let out a shout, jumped up, and got out of her seat and said, "Ronnie, I can't believe you would do that!"

Everyone began laughing at me, and I felt very embarrassed as I had not done anything. It was a setup from the beginning. The intention being to humiliate me. A very cruel thing to do indeed. But I had fell for it and felt like a fool. I was in fact, "somebody's fool."

My days at junior high school were some of the happiest days in my life. I had three very good friends there, Judy, Caroline, and Bonnie.

I enjoyed being with them so much. I was the shoulder they would cry on. We had lunch together almost every day at the drug store on Broadway, which had a soda fountain and booths to sit in. Junior High School was in the Schultz School building at that time, just a few blocks from Broadway.

One of our favorite things, was the cherry and chocolate syrup cokes. We only had about twenty minutes to spend there, so I would get there early to save us a booth. I was able to do this as I was a hall supervisor, and I got out of class early to monitor the halls, making sure no one was running instead of walking when they got out for lunch.

The problem was, I wasn't there to monitor the halls because I was saving us a booth at the drug store.

Sometimes another girl named Carolyn would come and have lunch with us. I felt different about this Carolyn than I did about my three buddies previously mentioned. I thought I loved her.

One day the girls asked me to play some songs on the juke box. Elvis Presley's song "Love Me Tender," was a big hit at the time and it was one of the songs I played. Almost as soon as the record began to play. Carolyn, the one whom I loved, began to cry profusely.

The other three girls and I all asked what was wrong, but she refused to tell us. Later, I discovered it reminded her of a boy whom she thought she loved, and the relationship had not worked out the way she had planned. She, too, was somebody's fool.

In my early years of high school, basketball games were popular and not always because we enjoyed watching the game. Several of us students played a game of our own outside, while the game inside went on.

It was called, "Hide and Catch." Here is how it was played. The boys would go hide, and if the girls found them they would get a kiss. Sometimes it was the other way around, and the girls would hide while the boys looked for them.

I thought this was a game I could get into, so I began to join them in this activity. It didn't take me long to notice however, that I was doing a very good job of hiding as the girls were never finding me. When I went to find them, someone had found them already.

This trend continued until I figured out that I was the only one who wasn't hooked up with a partner in the first place. I didn't know I needed one, I thought it was a free for all. Somebody was somebody's fool, I'm not sure yet as to who was the fool in this situation.

The time I felt the biggest fool of all was when I was around 18 years old. I was very much in love with a girl whom I was dating on a regular basis, almost steady. I say almost because once in awhile she was known to date someone else. I never knew who that someone was.

This girl and I often went to the Blue Hole Barbecue out on Kingshighway in my Chevy, which I was proud of. One day, in the middle of the week, my brother asked me if he could have my car for the evening. He had just begun driving, and why I agreed to let him borrow the car I shall never understand. Nevertheless, I did.

My cousin Larry dropped by that evening and asked me if I would like to bum around with him for a while, since I didn't have my car. I agreed, as I was at a loss on what to do without a car and this girl whom I was so in love with told me she had other plans.

My cousin asked me what I would like to do, and then suggested we could go to the Blue Hole Barbecue and have one of their great sandwiches. When we arrived my cousin asked me, "Is that your car sitting over there." I looked in the direction he was pointing to and sure enough, it was my car.

My car, my brother, and my girl!

I could not believe he would do such a thing. Then he added pain to my misery by going inside and playing a popular song in that day, on the juke box, which could be heard in the parking area, "Everybody's Somebody's Fool." I think it was sung by Connie Francis. I asked my cousin to take me home, where I laid on my bed and spent the rest of the evening crying, I was hurt, and I wasn't sure whom I should be mad at, my brother, my girl, or myself for being such a fool. I suppose, "Everybody's Somebody's Fool." By the way, my brother, I still love you!

(A personal note from the writer)

This month marks the third anniversary of my column "Written From The Heart," with the TBY. It was August 1995 my first article appeared "Lessons a Husband Must Learn." I would like to take this opportunity to express my sincere gratitude for the love and support I have received from my family in writing this column. My wife has shared me with my computer many a night as I spent countless hours writing articles for this column. I would also like to thank my daughter, Donna, for proofreading all of my columns. My wife, along with my children, my mother, and my brother, Dan and two sisters, have been very understanding about me sharing personal stories about my past, which at times involved them, thus finding themselves in my articles. Having a writer in your family who writes about his past life experiences is not always a cup of tea. Seldom is one consulted for permission to be included in a story such as this. To do so would bind the hands and heart of the writer to such an extent that he would lose the freedom to bear his soul before his readers and relate his thoughts and convictions.

Once again, I wish to thank you each and everyone, for being so understanding and giving me the joy of writing articles from the heart. I would also like to give a heart felt thanks to Marjorie Holmes, who was the inspiration for this wonderful column.

106

Lyrics Captured True Meaning of Our Freedom

I enjoyed the letter Bruce Collier sent concerning freedom. His letter embraces the following thoughts I have intended to share with your readers.

For decades, the 1960 hit song "Bobbie Magee" has replayed in my mind. Each time Janis Joplin sang the famous words "Freedom's just another word for nothing left to lose" I failed to see the forest for the trees. I always thought this statement was a rebellious put-down on freedom. It is, in fact, the most accurate truth concerning freedom one might find.

I am as proud and grateful as anyone for those who have fought and given their lives to keep our country free. I am proud to live in America. Nevertheless, I agree with Collier that the term "freedom" has taken on a new definition. Today, freedom is the password that opens the door to actions and lifestyles which lead to sin and bondage.

True freedom is found when one can say to God, "I surrender all." Freedom's just another word for nothing left to lose. He whom the son of God sets free is free indeed.

107

With All That Time, Just Stay Busy

I have noticed how strange the weather pattern has been, and I wonder if this could be a sign that the end is near.

I have listened to the news reporting about how too good to be true the economy is. Does this mean we are on the brink of a sudden stock market crash?

I have considered the increase in crime, teenagers becoming killers, the fact that drugs are abounding. Could it be that the Lord is preparing to strike down his right arm of judgement on this nation?

I have been a spectator to banks buying banks, each merger getting larger, and I have speculated about the possibility of a one-world government on the horizon.

I have observed there are people claiming to be God, wars and rumors of wars, famines and earthquakes in various places. And technology is increasing at the speed of light.

Being filled with anxiety about all of these things, I was led to ask God, "What does my awareness of all this mean?"

The Lord, quick to answer, said to me, "Your awareness of all these things means you have far too much time on your hands. Don't worry. Be busy."

108

Coffee, Cake—Stirring in My Heart

Food, a much talked about subject, and a subject that has given me an idea for a few stories, while dwelling upon what I should feed my tummy, as I feed my heart.

Coffee and Lessons Learned

As I was enjoying my morning cup of coffee, I began to recollect two important lessons I learned concerning this popular brewed beverage.

When I was 21 years of age, I took my first voyage out of Missouri, by rail, on a train, to sunny California. I looked young for my age, and the passengers on the train kept warning me to be cautious of the people out west, who would try to con me out of my money. I assured them I would be very careful.

As soon as I stepped off the train, an old man wearing shabby clothing walked up to me and asked, "Would you have a quarter to spare for a cup of coffee and a doughnut?" Remembering what I had been told on the train, I answered, "Sorry, I don't have a quarter to spare." The old man then asked, "Where are you from?" Knowing that he had never heard of my town since this was before Rush Limbaugh became famous, I informed him I was from Cape Girardeau, Missouri.

"I know where Cape Girardeau is," he quickly responded, "That's near Jackson, where I used to live." This took me by surprise. "You lived in Jackson, Missouri?" I asked. "I sure did," he said with a grin on his unshaven face. He extended his hand to shake mine and said, "Say young man, how about helping a neighbor from Missouri with a quarter for a doughnut and a cup of coffee?"

I reached in my pocket and pulled out a quarter. While looking ever so slowly at the portrait of George Washington on the coin, who according to legend never told a lie, I placed the quarter in the old man's hand. As I did so, I even felt guilty for telling him I didn't have a quarter to spare when in truth I did.

A few years later, I learned that there is at least one city or town named Jackson in every state in the Union. How was I to know? I had never been any farther from Cape Girardeau than Saint Louis. I thought Jackson, Missouri, was the only city named Jackson. How else would he have known about a city just eight miles from Cape, if he had not lived there?

Lets Go Dutch!

As a student at the Cape Girardeau beauty school, I had the opportunity to shampoo the hair of some very important people. The shampoo I recall the best was with Mrs. Rust, mother of Gary Rust. I felt honored to have been trusted with such an important client, and we had a nice conversation as I washed her hair. Mrs. Rust was a pleasant and easy person to converse with. I asked her why her son Gary had left politics to work full-time with his newspaper business.

The question evidently stirred up some strong feelings, as she lifted her head up and out of the shampoo bowl and said to me, "Why you wouldn't believe what it is like in that city!" Referring to Washington, D.C., she continued, "You cannot let a person buy you a cup of coffee in that town without them expecting a favor in return." With that being said, we began talking about other things, which was probably the right thing for us to do.

I have tried to rationalize feeling obligated to someone for buying me a cup of coffee, since the day Mrs. Rust confided that story to me. A cup of coffee doesn't seem like much of a bribe. Nevertheless, when a person is ready to draw the line, by refusing to accept so much as a cup of coffee, in order to remain honest and not obligated, I would say he is a person whom I would consider to be trustworthy.

In conclusion, the moral of this story is never believe someone when they say they're from Jackson, and if someone offers to buy you a cup of coffee, go Dutch!

The Analogy of the Cake and the Child

Once upon a time (most stories begin this way) a lady made a cake with the utmost of care. She carefully inserted all the right ingredients necessary to have a really good cake.

It was not a small effort she made. It was to be her prize cake. She gave much attention to every detail, and was absolutely, positively certain, that this was a blue ribbon cake. She took the cake to the county fair, thus sending it out into the world, to be tested and tasted by those whom she knew, and by those she knew not.

Then something strange happened. No great reviews were coming back to her concerning her cake. In fact, it was leaving a bad taste in a lot of people's mouths. It had lost its flavor and seemed to be crumbling apart. She was sure she had made it right, and had put in all the right ingredients. How could such a thing happen? It was as if the cake had a mind of its own, and had tossed out all of those important ingredients for texture and strength and flavor.

So it was not consumed as it drifted from one county fair to another. After several days, as it had aged, the cake returned to her home. She was bewildered by what she found. Instead of turning green with mold, the cake seemed to be regaining its beauty. It had become a firm, strong cake, and the ingredients once so carefully inserted, began to show their worth. Its flavor had improved daily, and it was now certainly clear—it was becoming the blue ribbon cake she intended it to be.

How strange is the resemblance of this cake story with the story of her one and only child.

She had brought a child into the world, and she had raised it with the utmost care. Everything she had learned and every experience others had learned and gave her for advice, she used to raise this child.

This child was to become her trophy, to look at and admire. She taught the child every moral value she had learned as a child. She gave her child an education and all the wisdom she could muster, so this child would be a stronger, wiser individual.

Then came the day to send her child out into the world. To be tasted and tested by those she knew and those she knew not. Then something strange happened.

Her child was not achieving the greatness she once thought was certain. The people who called her about her child were not calling to compliment.

Her child was leaving a bad taste and a trail of heartache for many, including the one who brought this youngster into the world. The child's life seemed to be falling apart—crumbling so to speak. She pondered what went wrong. She knew she had raised the child right, with the right moral and ethical values. It was as if everything she taught the child was dismissed and discarded, considered by the child as worthless and unnecessary.

Although death and poverty knocked on the child's door many times, the person was never totally consumed. As the child drifted from one place to another over the years, the mother began observing a bewildering change. Her child seemed to be regressing to the values she had been taught early in her life. Her child was becoming more mature, happy, successful. Actually, an adult this child had become. And when the child came home to visit, this was clear. Her child would most certainly become that trophy to look at and admire, the blue ribbon for her to cherish and love, and be proud of. Thus ends the story of the analogy of the cake and the child.

Words are but food for thought. This column was more about thoughts than food. As food is for the body, thoughts are for the mind. One should observe closely, and give much consideration before partaking foods or thoughts. I sincerely hope you have found these thoughts agreeable and digestible.

109

Long Distance Not Like It Used to be

When I received my telephone bill this morning, there was a $135 charge for long-distance calls. I was billed for 49 calls made to 15 states over a period of 24 days—calls I did not make. I was billed by a billing service I had never heard of before which told me to call a long-distance company I had never heard of before. The long-distance company informed me it had never heard of me before, but it would try to figure out who made these calls. Then it asked me to call the telephone company and seek mercy in not paying for the charges until the research was completed. It appears making long-distance calls has become too convenient for slick operators instead of telephone operators.

Whatever happened to the good old days when you were lucky enough to get on your phone before the other party began using it? You remember, don't you, when everyone had a black phone with a wheel of fortune on the face of it, and let your fingers do the twist? Sometimes you twisted your fingers until you couldn't get them out.

Those were the days when you talked to a real person and not a computer voice, and the real person would go the ends of the Earth to reach the party you wished to speak to. Then she listened in on what you were going to say after you made your call. That was when long-distance calling was something you rarely thought of, but when you did it was a big event.

I remember my father making such a long-distance call once. Almost. He needed to speak to someone who lived out of state about an urgent matter and did not know the person's phone number. So with his four children at his feet and his wife by his side, he dialed the operator. I almost forgot. There was also our dog, Lady, watching with wonder. He told us to be very quiet, as this was really important, and sometimes it was difficult to hear the operator. My father

225

had never before attempted this feat before, and when the operator came on and asked what he needed, I could sense he was a bit more than nervous.

He informed the operator he needed the person's number, and she informed him to stay on the phone while she searched for it. We played quietly on the floor, as did Lady, for what seemed to be forever. Finally I heard my father say, "Yes, Operator, I am still here," as he asked my mom to get him a piece of paper and a pen. It was also at that moment someone began knocking at our door, and Lady, being the watchdog of our house, began barking loudly letting us know someone was there.

My father, still nervous and wanting to hear the operator, turned to our dog and said, "Lady, shut your mouth!" When the operator heard my father shout this into the phone's receiver, she replied, "Very well, you can get the phone number yourself!"

110

The Future Depends on God's Will

To see the hope for the future through the eyes of a high school or college student, in my humble opinion, would be either a foolish wish made in vain or a great illusion of deceit, unless that hope was placed in God's word. Consider, if you will, what the world has to offer a young person with a dream and what message it has portrayed in recent years.

A young person hears every day the message of materialism and that the substance is the measure of a successful life. Every advertisement confirms this blatant false conception. To acquire this substance, immediate credit is made available with a plastic card which bears the name of a person who is soon to become the slave to the one who issued the card. The concept of paying for needs by hard, honest work as one has the ability to do so and being willing to patiently wait for things until they can be paid for has been replaced with "Enjoy your heart's desires now" and pay for the rest of your life the penalty for that immediate self-gratification. One enslaved to credit card debt has no hope.

A young person hears every day that a good self-esteem is available to one who esteems oneself above anything that says he is anything but perfect. He is told that he has complete control over his destiny. He is told that every choice he makes can be the right choice, because right and wrong values are only worthy of the one who makes the decision. This road of thinking leads to a multitude of detour signs which go unheeded and ends on a dead end street of disaster. Hope is not found here.

As adults and parents who have come through the trials and tribulations of the world's deceit, we face a great responsibility in sharing the truth of where hope can be found for future generations. We must plead for our children to seek the return of biblical principles to govern our country.

I conclude with the words of Alexis de Tocqueville, French statesman, historian and social philosopher who traveled to America in the 1830s to discover the reason for the incredible success of this new nation, from his classic "Democracy in America."

"I sought for the key to greatness and genius of America in her harbors, in her fertile fields and boundless forests, in her rich mines and vast world commerce, in her public school system and institutions of learning. I sought for it in her democratic Congress and in her matchless Constitution.

"Not until I went into the churches of America and heard her pulpits flame with righteousness did I understand the secret of her genius and power.

"America is great because America is good, and if America ever ceases to be good, America will cease to be great."

111

Chicago—Near My Home Town

In the late '50s and very early '60s, the long arm of the gang mob in Chicago reached the Illinois side of the river directly across from Cape Girardeau in what is known as Southern Illinois. The gang activity was being funneled by owners of large night clubs and vending machine operations. Night clubs had continuous strip shows, and opportunities for small bands to take their place on the stages of these clubs were plentiful.

Gambling operations, as in Las Vegas and now on river boats, however, were illegal to the best of my knowledge. I have never told anyone the things I observed as a young teenager, playing music in a band in some of those clubs. I was afraid to tell anyone, especially my mom and dad. They would have never permitted me to cross the river again if they had known of some situations I encountered. More than likely, many would never have believed me.

Most of all, I feared for my life. Had I ratted on some crime figure who ran operations in Cairo, or perhaps even closer to my hometown such as Mclure, Ill., I might have met a fate that would have kept me from writing this column.

So, you might be asking yourself why now? Nearly 40 years have passed and I suspect that most of those involved have passed away, been murdered, or have grown too old to care. Nevertheless, I intend to tread very lightly, and change every name if I mention a name, and even change the exact location to protect myself and those who may be innocent—and those who claim innocence because it was never proven otherwise.

I hope you find the stories interesting, and if you suspect I have a wild imagination and these are only my fantasies, that's ok, I won't mind, and I am sure there are others who won't mind either. In fact, they are probably counting on it!

What's Going on Behind the Green Door?

It was a Friday evening and I had been asked to join a band for a music gig. We were on our way to one of the largest night clubs in Southern Illinois. It seemed like a long drive getting there; however, in those days on two-lane highways it seemed a long time getting anywhere. As we approached the club, I was amazed at the number of automobiles already in the parking lot. We had a crowd and hadn't even set our equipment on the stage yet!

"This was going to be good," raced through my mind. There must have been at least 50 cars parked on that lot. The club was owned by a juke box operation owner and there were rumors he had ties with the Chicago mob.

When we left Cape to play this job, I was a bit hesitant to play in a club owned by a known gangster. Now, however, I was thinking this was pretty cool—they get a lot of customers.

As we entered the door with our equipment in hand, I was shocked! Where were the people? The only person I saw was the bartender behind the bar, and a guy looking through a glass window in the green door that was in the back of the club. I prematurely concluded that perhaps everybody is back there eating dinner and will be coming out to hear us play.

We set up our instruments and began playing at nine o'clock. We played for 45 minutes to a huge dance floor, surrounded by tables covered with white table cloths, and one person—the guy behind the bar. It was the topic of discussion as we sat around a table on our first break. Where were the people? Who is this guy who keeps looking through the green door? Were we just a front for something going on in that room?

At the end of our break, we started playing our second set. A man came in and sat at the bar. Finally, we had at least one person who would listen to us play. But not for long. He appeared to be having quite a conversation with the bartender, and when he was served his second drink he fell off the bar stool onto the floor.

We thought the man had a heart attack or was sick, so we stopped playing and walked toward the bar. The man behind the green door came out and also walked to the bar. The bartender and the other man took out his wallet and mentioned who and what he was. I can't reveal this information, but he was not a dog collector, let me tell you!

They grabbed one of his arms and dragged him outside. We followed. The owner of the club came outside and talked to the two who had dragged out the intruder. He then put on what was known in those days as brass knuckles. And as the two workers held the state inspector in a standing position, the owner began pounding him all over his body. After about three minutes of this abuse they put him in the trunk of a car, and another man drove the car away. I never saw that man again!

We returned to the stage, shaken and shocked, and tried to finish the job. After our four-hour session, with no more people visible the entire night, we took our band instruments and loaded them in the car, and headed back to the calmness of our city, Cape Girardeau. It was a first for all of us. We didn't talk about it on the way home. We never talked about it to anyone, anytime, never!

"In the Foggy Air"

I have room for one more tale if I keep it short. I was playing with a band in Cairo at a place we'll call Club 13, on 13th Street. We were on a break and talking to "pork chops," a bartender and bouncer there. The phone rang behind the bar, and as "pork chops" spoke to someone he wrote down a message. When he hung up the phone he asked me and another band member if we would like to take a ride with him, as he had a message to deliver. We told him "Sure, why not!"

Pork chops and my friend sat in the front seat as I crawled in the back. When we got on the highway, it was so foggy you couldn't see 10 feet. I thought we were traveling at a high speed and I leaned over the front seat to see how fast we were going. The needle was pegged at the 100-mile-an-hour mark. The fog was so thick you couldn't cut it with a power saw.

After 20 minutes we began slowing down as if Pork Chops knew where we were. I don't know how he knew, as one could not see a thing on the side of the road. We pulled in a gravel driveway, which lead to a wooden shed with two large doors. Pork Chops dimmed his lights off and on, then turned them off and on as if he was giving a signal in Morse code. Suddenly, a man came out of the shed wearing a suit with a necktie, and a hat that was slightly slanted toward one side. He had a mustache, and he held his right hand inside the left side of his suit coat, as if he was going to draw a gun.

He was standing directly in front of the car with the lights on. Pork Chops gave him the piece of paper and we drove back to the club the way we came—100 miles an hour in the fog. No one asked what was on that note, nor who was the man in the double-breasted suit. I always thought that he was a hit man, and he was receiving information on his next hit. What would you have thought? I mean the guy looked like a bad guy in a Dick Tracy movie.

I never found out who or what he was, but I did see him again, or at least someone who could have been his twin, 30 years later in a restaurant having dinner with a lady I presumed was his wife. Right here in my hometown, which was at one time, near Chicago.

112

Lessons in Life for Car and It's Owner

This last week has been quite an experience in life for me and my old car, Old red. Last week, Old Red was sitting at a four-way stop being mannerly and waiting his turn. All of a sudden a huge, yellow fellow named John Deere came up behind him and hit him with a 6-foot-in-diameter concrete collar. Needless to say, it knocked the glass out his back window and inserted a nasty dent in his trunk.

Just four days later, I was in the hospital having about the same thing happen to me. I had a colonoscopy. A single polyp was previously discovered, and the objective was to remove it. In doing so, seven polyps were discovered and removed. Thus, Old Red and I both experienced quite a trauma. Now we are waiting for a verdict. Will we be totaled and considered a complete loss, or will we be considered for future opportunities to contribute to this world we are in.

We have discovered, Old Red and I, that waiting for a verdict is an extremely frightening thing one has to sometimes do. There is one verdict, however, for human beings that can be assured before the day of judgment. God says in his word he will accept and acquit us—declare us not guilty—if we trust Jesus Christ to take away our sins. Yes, all have sinned and fall short of God's glory. But because of his unlimited grace, we can find forgiveness through Jesus Christ; who freely takes away our sin.

113

Great Physician Heals Those Who Show Faith

Many of you have heard the song "It is No Secret What God Can Do." It continues, "What he has done for others, he will do for you."

These words ring with a glorious truth. God, will do for others what he has done for you. So when God does something for you, you need to let others know he will do it for them. Thus the reason for this letter.

Everyone, it seems, has been having sore throats along with infected ears. Trips to the doctor's office and taking medicine have helped some, but not all. So when my ears began to give me much pain and my throat became sore, I turned to my No. 1 physician, Jesus. I said, "Lord, I know you can heal me, and I know that you want to." I then continued with a statement that even surprised me. "Lord I know that you will." I immediately felt the pain leave me, and I knew in my heart the reason why. I had pleased the Lord with my faith statement.

It is not difficult to believe the Lord can heal us, nor is it hard to believe he wants to. Most of us, including me, have trouble sometimes believing that he will. If you need a miracle from God, affirm these truths. I know that you can. I know that you want to. And I know that you will. What he did for me, he will do for you.

114

Those Are the Moments to Remember

I sometimes find it difficult to live in these times. I am convinced that the reason I find it arduous, is this excellent memory I possess. I can remember how good life was 30 to 40 years ago—a time when life moved at a slower pace, and when there were fewer people involved in that pace. Looking to the past, to recall the moments of how life was, I have discovered "these are the moments to remember."

When Coke was the Real Thing!

I can remember when a coke, for the price of a nickel, came in a glass bottle. I recall when the taste of this soft drink left a tingling sensation in your mouth. It contained enough acid to cut the salt off of peanuts in seconds, eat a copper penny overnight, and stimulate your brain for hours upon end. I can remember when Coke was the real thing.

When Movies were a Social Event!

I can recall when going to a movie cost a quarter or a dime on bargain night. For that price you were offered two movies, cartoons, and news briefs as to what was happening around the world. You could stay for as long as you wanted, and be totally uninhibited with your date—if you had one. If you didn't have a date, you could often find one sitting nearby. This was the primary reason for most young people being there to begin with. Buying soda and popcorn, placed no heavy burden on your pocket change back then, and one could even buy chewing gum, which was usually disposed of on the bottom side of the seat.

When Fruit and Veggies were Free!

In the heart of the city there were large yards for children to play in, with gardens producing vegetables far better than what's found in the stores today. I can recall grapevines loaded with grapes on fences, and fruit trees for children to pick from when hungry. Food tasted better back then, before microwaves, frozen foods, and everything made instant. It was worth waiting for, and the wait seemed no longer than what we experience today.

When Cars and Toys were Indestructible!

Scooters and three-wheelers were made of hard metal, as were the toys a child would play with. Toy planes, trains and even piggy banks were made of cast iron or something similar. I can remember when automobiles were made like an army tank, fancied with chrome, and spacious inside. You could sit in any position you desired in those cars, and most every position imaginable was attempted in those days.

The automobiles had engines you could recognize when lifting the hood, and most of the time one could determine, without a computer, what the problem was. They used more gasoline I will admit, but gas was a quarter or a dime a gallon during a gas war. And when you bought that gas, they gave you full service with a friendly smile. They checked your oil, your radiator, the air in your tires, and made sure your windows were clean.

When Daily Chores Kept You Fit!

I can remember when there was no need for exercise tapes and walks at the mall. A person would get all the exercise they needed doing their daily chores. When lawns were mowed by a push mower and one's arms and legs powered them instead of an engine. When the fuel for the fire was delivered by trips from the basement, or wherever the buckets of coal was stored. When walking to one's destination was most often expected and not considered an effort of sacrifice. This was city living, one can only imagine the physical effort that was exerted on a farm.

When Spending a Dollar, Didn't Make You Scream!

I have written before about the 10 factor. How everything you buy today will cost you about 10 times as much as it did back then. It is difficult to forget the price you paid for items in those days. When my wife and I got married, I bought furniture for a three-room apartment—a living room, bedroom, and kitchen. We bought furniture for all three rooms for the price most folks now pay for a sofa or a chair.

The cost of living 30 years ago was not out of line with the income one made. It was even better 40 years ago. It was a time when you got paid every Friday, not every two weeks or once a month. When you could charge your groceries to your account until the end of the week, because you and the owner had a personal friendly relationship. It was the same at the bank. If you needed a loan, you could walk in and ask to speak to the president or vice president. They knew you by your first name, and were more than happy to work with you.

If you had a phone, you got charged for one thing—having a phone. There were no trash bills. You just disposed of it in a metal barrel in the back yard, or piled it up and buried it. No cable TV bills—rabbit ears worked fine. Now it seems every bill you get has federal, state and local taxes, or a finance charge on it.

115

So Much to Do With so Little Time Left to Do It

Recently a co-worker celebrated his birthday where I work. It was his 37th birthday. I told him I had been married for almost that number of years and it made me feel old. He looked at me with the most serious expression I have ever observed and said, "Ron, you are old."

This caused me to give thought to the subject of my age. Was it true? Had I became an old person? Before the day was over I found myself having a conversation with another co-worker who has lived as long as I have plus a year or two. "Do you find it amazing how fast the years have gone," I asked. He looked at me with the same expression I had seen that morning and said, "If you want to put it into perspective, think about this: You and I have 20 more summers."

Twenty more summers to live, I pondered, and even that is not certain. Years pass like turning a page in a book, and they slip away like grasping a handful of oil. Then this undeniable truth hit me: How little I have done with the years I have had, and how little I am doing with the time I have now. I heard myself praying, "God forgive me, and show me this day the work you would have me to do."

116

Holy Word Offers Hope

Recently after a church service I pondered as to why so many Bibles have black covers. I said to God, "Lord, black is a color which makes one think of death, and black represents darkness. Why is this color used to cover your word?" He replied, "To send this message: In the midst of darkness there is life, my living Word. In the midst of darkness there is hope, love, a place of refuge for one's soul when experiencing the outer darkness of a sinful world."

How beautiful and wonderful is God's love for us.

How great is his wisdom to place these treasures where we will need them the most: "In the midst of darkness."

117

Close Encounter of a Heavenly Kind

It was warm for an October evening, as I walked with my three children from our house to the supermarket. My wife had asked for ice cream, and the kids were excited to be going with their dad to the store, rather than being sent to bed.

The bright lights, which normally give the parking lot behind our home a daytime appearance, were dimmer than ususal, and I wondered if there might be a light fog in the air. As we walked by the long white fence behind our home that leads to the sidewalk, I caught a vision of something flying directly over our heads. It was about six to seven feet above us.

At first I thought it was a thick, low-flying cloud. Then it appeared to be shaped like a man. Stranger still, it had wings like a bird. As it swiftly flew over us, it also flew over the roof of the grocery store we were approaching.

I shouted to my children, "Did you guys see that?" They responded with, "See what daddy, what did you see?" As we crossed the street to the store I attempted to describe what I had seen. It was like something out of a Superman movie I kept thinking. Was it a bird, a plane?

We entered the store and I made an effort to put what had just happened our of my mind. The kids were in a joyous mood that night, and I didn't want to make them afraid. I told them I would buy them each a treat of their choice, so we began our search up and down the aisles.

I kept having this overpowering feeling I was being observed. It was not a fearful feeling, but I knew that my every step and movement was being watched, and it was distracting me from the children's questions. This concerned them and they asked if something was wrong. I assured them everything was all right, and that I was just thinking about what I had seen.

We found the ice cream for my wife, the kids had their treats in hand, and we left the store for home on the same path we came. My oldest child, Kristy, who was 10 years old at the time, with the youngest being three, was always the most inquisitive of the three children. Thus it came as no surprise when she began firing questions about what I thought I had seen.

"What do you think it was daddy, do you think we will see it too?" I smiled at her and said, "If you look believing you will see it, then you will!" I don't know why I answered her that way, except that it sounded biblical, and I was very much into reading the Bible for the past several months.

It was three months prior to this night when I had been supernaturally healed of alcoholism while reading the Bible. A few weeks after this healing had taken place, I received the baptism of the Holy Spirit and began speaking in a language which I had never spoken before nor currently understand. Of this I knew, God had been working miracles in my life, and had restored my life and my relationship with him, my wife and my children. For me, this was all that really mattered.

So with belief in her heart, Kris and my other two children began searching the sky believing they would see what daddy had seen. Suddenly Kris, with excitement in her voice, said, "Look daddy, is that what you saw?"

We had just turned the corner of the white fence at the back of our yard and she was pointing toward the sky. When I looked where she was pointing, I was amazed. It appeared to be balls of fire with tails blazing through the air toward our home. As our eyes followed them, seven large lamps circular in shape formed a triangle. We stood in awe.

The triangle appeared to be 50 feet in the sky and in front of us, which would put it directly over the top of the police station parking lot across from the front of our house. I recall very little conversation between the children and myself, as we stood with our mouths wide open.

I do remember telling Kristy to go inside and tell her mother to come out and see it. She returned saying mom didn't want to come out as she was watching TV. This came as no surprise as she never did give much credit to things of a supernatural nature, and she had always felt my imagination was only exceeded by those of our children. Besides, she wanted to dig into that ice cream we had just brought home.

As the kids and I continued to stare at this sign against the darkness of the sky, it was as if time stood still. I remember the four of us holding hands as we watched it but we did not feel fearful, just totally amazed. I don't know how long we watched it, but suddenly one of the seven circles left the formation and came directly over our heads—as if to say goodbye—then returned to the others and all of them took off with supersonic speed in different directions and disappeared.

Immediately a car pulled up in front of the house. It was a nephew whom I had been praying for and whom I had asked the Lord to deliver into my hands if he became suicidal. I had also asked the Lord to give me a sign indicating that my nephew needed help. Now it all seemed to make sense.

The cloud that appeared as a man was no doubt an angel who was keeping guard over my steps before the arrival of the sign. The seven circles in the sky, in the shape of a triangle, was the sign of completeness, of the Lord delivering my nephew as I had asked. The eyes of the Lord kept us in waiting until my nephew was strongly encouraged by "something" he said, which told him to come to my house in his hour of despair.

My nephew now strongly serves the Lord, and has been set free of his depression. My children remember the event much like I, with different theories as to what it was that we had seen. Kristy feels it was a UFO. As for me, I will always believe what I know in my heart to be true. One October evening, my three children and I, had a close encounter—of a heavenly kind.

118

Frank Rayburn's Heart Reflects Love of God

I was surprised to see a picture of Frank Rayburn, a very dear friend of mine, in an article concerning organ transplants. The article said Frank had received a heart. Upon reading this, my thoughts took me back to my grade-school days when Frank and I became acquainted. The thing I remembered about Frank more than anything else was the love and kindness that came from his heart. We have crossed paths over the years, and Frank still has that heart of flesh, and I am so glad this is possible. This gift has extended his life. And for those of us who love him, this gives us more opportunities to feel the love God has for us which is reflected in the heart of Frank Rayburn.

119

Jesus' Precept: Less Judging and More Love

Much has been said in recent days about being judgmental of others, such as how one should dress in church. God's Word is very clear about the subject of judging one another, as it is about the subject of our need to love one another.

I recently read the following from a pastor's sermon notes. Jesus walked with the disciples through good times and bad times, during picnics and in the middle of storms. When they failed him, when they denied him, he reached out to them to help them continue to walk with him.

What a powerful love he had for them, and it is his desire and commandment that we love one another as he loves us.

Let us walk together in love and stop judging one another.

120

The Splendid Days of Grand Parenting

I have some good stories about the things grandchildren say and how inquisitive their little minds can be.

Do They Have Cherry Cobbler in Heaven?

A friend whom I occasionally see recently lost her husband. Her 4-year-old grandson, being told his grandpa had gone to a place called Heaven, had many questions about this place. One evening she and her grandson were making a cherry cobbler together.

"Do they have cherry cobbler in heaven, Grandma?" Her grandson asked. "I'm sure they do," she replied. After the cherry cobbler was made, she put it in the refrigerator to cool and informed her grandson they could have some the next day.

Later that evening the thought of having a small dish of the cobbler sounded like an excellent idea, but she remembered she had told her grandson they should wait until the next day to eat it.

The next morning, when her grandson climbed out of bed, he ran to the refrigerator to look at the cobbler. "Grandma, Grandma," he shouted, "you were right!"

"I was right about what?" my friend asked.

"They must have cherry cobbler in Heaven like you said," he exclaimed. "It's still all here and Grandpa didn't need to eat a single bite!"

Up, Up and Away

Another friend of mine has two granddaughters who lost their father at an early age. They had both been told that their daddy was in Heaven.

On their daddy's birthday they bought him some helium balloons, and they wanted to release them and watch them fly toward Heaven and their daddy. As my friend watched them play with the balloons, she thought perhaps they would enjoy keeping them.

"You don't have to let the balloons fly away," she told them, "Daddy knows you bought them for him, and he wouldn't care if you kept them."

Nevertheless, the two girls wanted to do what they had intended. They went to a field and held out their balloons, wished their daddy a happy birthday, and kept their eyes on the balloons until they were out of sight. As I was told this story, I felt a flood of emotions fill my soul. I also sensed a feeling of confidence that went farther than a hunch, that the girls' father received those balloons, and was smiling down in love.

What Does a Granny Sound Like?

When my grandson had just learned to talk, we were testing his intelligence on how to make different sounds.

"What does a dog sound like?" we asked him. "Bark! Bark!" my grandson replied, with a facial expression that reflected his pride in knowing the answer.

"What does a cat sound like?" We asked him. "Meow, meow," my grandson quickly said back.

We gave him an applause and said words of praise such as "You are such a smart little boy!" Then came the difficult question, "What does a granny sound like?"

We waited as he gave it a second of thought and then he said, "No. No. No."

The Days of French Fries and Ketchup

Recently, I observed an event that has been a reoccurring scene in my mind. I credit this to the impact it made in my heart when I observed it, and that it took me back in time to when my two daughters were still "daddy's little girls."

I was having coffee early that morning in a favorite fast-food restaurant for kids. At a table close by was a father and his two darling daughters. I would guess the girls to be about three and five. As I wondered where the mother might be, I couldn't help but notice what a delightful time the father and his daughters were sharing. "How sweet," I thought, their dad has taken them out for a special breakfast, or perhaps it was the other way around. It brought back memories of when my two daughters were about that age. As I continued to look their way, I noticed how they admired their dad. It was, "Daddy is this the way you put ketchup on your fries?" And, "Daddy, did you drink orange juice when you were a kid?"

They looked at him as if he was the only man in the world. He was giving them the same attention. He was at their rescue with a paper napkin before they had a chance to ask for one. He was filling their ketchup cups like he did it for a living, and he was enjoying it. He was their hero, their knight in shining armor.

I found it a beautiful sight to behold. I had been there, done that. I began thinking about what was to come for that father in the years ahead, as his two daughters became teenagers and then young ladies. He would most likely be fine until his girls reached their teens. However, he would notice his wallet making more trips out of his pocket for the things they would need.

The real pain will begin when they start giving their attention to another. In the years ahead they will find a boy to eat French fries and ketchup with. The dad will feel like a jilted lover. Left alone and deserted, his shining armor tarnished, he might possibly feel jealous. Where once upon a time it was his daughters who sought his attention, now he discovers it is he who finds it almost impossible to get theirs.

In the meantime, his wallet has not slowed down any in making those trips from his pocket to their hand. In fact, it seems the trips are on the increase, as is the amount being removed.

As the father grows with wisdom, he will begin to see the value of his girls finding someone else attractive. Someone who might be willing to remove their wallet to buy those French fries. I realized the father had a lot of life's lessons in the years ahead. Still, those were the days—the days of French fries and ketchup—and these are the days of our lives.

121

Life as We Would Write It Would be Fairy Tale

If we could write the story of our life and live it out the way we wrote it, instead of living our life and then writing a story about it, how different a life we would live, and how different a story one would read.

Our life's story would be of a life that never felt pain nor experienced the loss of a loved one. It would be a life where every decision and every action we took was for the good of everyone. Our life would be one of love, peace and harmony, not bound by doubt nor fear and filled with joy and happiness each and every day.

If we could write the story of our life and then live it, life would be a fairy tale, and we would have never known life at all.

122

Death is No Longer a Stranger

Death was once such a stranger. I was introduced to this stranger at my grandfather's funeral. I wept as I observed the tears of sorrow being shed by those who were more aware of the loss of my grandfather than I was.

Then came the stranger's visitation to five classmates killed in a car crash, all in their teens. This gave a new meaning to death's expectation. Age was no longer a factor.

Thoughts of fate and circumstance and the life hereafter dominated the space in my mind reserved for searching for truth and wisdom. As years passed by like pages swiftly turning, friends and relatives who came to terms with this stranger increased exceedingly. The sudden appearance of this stranger to those whom I loved created regrets in my heart for words unspoken and deeds undone.

Thus, I found myself in prayer before the Lord. The thought has never occurred to me that I would pray for those who had crossed over to the other side. Nevertheless, I prayed that the Lord would, in his own way, express my love and good intentions which were cut short by this stranger.

True, I could no longer hold them in my arms, but I could hold them in my heart and in my prayers. Even then I knew that little by little I had to let them go. One cannot hold onto the past and make room for the future.

Then the stranger came to my father's door. My father did battle with him and chased him away more than once. The stranger persisted, however, and after many battles his persistence won. Fight and resist as one may, death is as certain as our need to know there is life after death.

Now my mother has passed away. But I have comfort, for now death is no longer a stranger. In fact, I know now death can be a friend. When these bodies which harbor our souls become like a worn out garment, one might call out to this friend who was once a foe and say, "I'm ready for the journey. I want to be with my friends and loved ones on the other side. I know where I am going, and death has lost its sting."

My mother viewed death in this manner. Her last gift to me was showing me there was nothing to fear, that there is a time to give up the battle and find that victory is the reward and gift which the Lord Jesus has given to those who believe in him. Death is not a stranger anymore.

123

Humorous Wit—The Key to Someone's Heart

I've been told that as a child, I was always saying things that made those around me laugh. Most certainly, everyone enjoys a good bout of laughter now and then. There is so little to laugh about anymore, or so it seems. Perhaps it's the way we look at things that determine their value in tears or joy.

Take the human body, for instance, that has surpassed the age of 40. One can look at the tube around the waist line or those extra saddle bags being carried on the behind side, and get really depressed. Or you can look in the mirror and laugh your head off at the reflection you're seeing.

For we both know there ain't no way the person in the mirror is the one standing in front of it. What happens to a mirror that reflects a person's body after 40? Mirrors do crazy things. Make a person look like they have wrinkles in their skin, less hair on their head. And teeth? Well, they just disappear sometimes. Mirrors do strange things to people after 40, but if you look at it in the right way, it's something to laugh about.

While we're on the subject of past 40, consider the humor of one's sex life. Believe it or not, you had one—once upon a time. The mind is a little foggy as to how or when, but those kids didn't happen by themselves. For many past 40, the wife has gone to the body shop and had some parts removed, and perhaps your energy has taken a downward turn.

Now a television has replaced what used to be, and a good book had become the release for the tension of the day. This would be depressing if you thought of how it used to be, but with the help of a memory loss, (one begins to experience at 40), and the right attitude, it's something to laugh about. At least I try!

Many things that at one time seemed frightening and anything but funny, become hilarious later in life. Permit me to give you an example:

My wife and I had been married for just over a year. We each owned a car—hers a small white one, mine a small yellow one. For some reason she took my car to work one day and left hers behind with me. I had a dental appointment that day, and I know of absolutely nothing that terrifies me more than sitting in a dental chair, having a tooth removed.

I kept my appointment and had my tooth removed, in spite of trying to fight my way out of that chair the entire time. I left with tears in my eyes, a jaw swollen up and feeling slightly numb. I got in my wife's car and headed for the beauty shop where she worked. I wanted to see if I could receive a little pity from that cute, red-haired wife of mine.

Traveling toward William Street, I caught a glimpse of what appeared to be my car. I turned my head in that direction and saw a blonde-haired lady driving my car! I turned my eyes back to the road in front of me, only to find a car had come to a dead stop. With no time for me to stop, I hit that car and put a dent in my wife's car.

I then got my very first traffic ticket—after 10 years of perfect driving. Deciding to limp my shattered spirit home along with my wife's wounded car, I noticed my car was already there when I arrived. I also noticed that my cute little red-haired wife was now a cute little blonde. Instead of having pity for me she was very hurt about what I had done to her car.

As I look back on this event, my wife coloring her hair, which caused me to wreck her car, seems funny. Really it does! I laugh inside every time I think about it.

My wife has a different reaction to this remembrance. She feels anger thinking about her little white car, which never had a dent until that day. If it had been my car, I would not likely find the memory of this event funny. I didn't find it funny at the time it happened. Now however, I can look on it with a humorous attitude.

A Special Valentine Message to My Wife

One enchanted evening, 32 years ago, I finally surrendered to my cousin's nagging, and agreed to a blind date with a girl whom he had met in St. Louis. He had been trying for months to get me to drive 125 miles to date her, but I firmly refused.

Looking my best, I drove to her address, walked up to the door and knocked once or twice. The door opened and there she stood. A beautiful young lady, her hair slightly frosted, dark brown eyes, which happened to be my favorite color.

She stood a foot shorter than me, making me feel tall for the first time in my life. It is hard to feel tall when you're five feet four. Our eyes met and I think at that moment she knew, I knew, and anyone who saw us together that night knew, it was a relationship made in heaven.

I was under her magic spell. She had grace, charm and charisma. She captivated my heart immediately. One year later we were married. Now after 32 years, I love her even more.

There has been tears, and there has been laughter. Most important of all, there has been love.

124

Rapture Movie is Must-See Film for Everyone

I am so proud of this newspaper and the coverage it provides. I was pleased to see the coverage concerning the movie "Left Behind." My family had an opportunity to view this movie prior to its appearance on the big screen. I wish to encourage you to see the movie. My wife and I were even more blessed this past Sunday as Pastor Gary Brothers spoke on "Rapture Realities." Is the rapture a reality? How does the rapture relate to me? These are some of the many questions Brothers answered in his sermon.

For many, the thought of people being caught up in the air by an unseen supernatural force is beyond their imagination. I am still amazed every time I observe a paper clip being lifted off the surface of a table by a magnet. Nevertheless, I have seen it happen time and time again: an unseen force lifting a metal object being caught up in the air to meet it. If a magnet can lift a paper clip, how can one not believe that God, who is the creator of this unseen force, can lift his children in the air to meet him?

125

Footprints in the Sand

The restaurant was rather empty, as my wife and I were being seated at our table. Nevertheless, the noise level was far conducive to a relaxing atmosphere.

There was a family of seven sitting at a large table nearby, and the conversation was being monopolized by one person. A rather obese man, about the age of 50, had a voice that reverberated throughout the entire seating area.

Under normal circumstances, I would be able to shut out this type of distraction and carry on my own conversation. However, this individual's character presented a strange attraction to me, so I listened and observed their dinner conversation.

He seemed to be in a joyous mood, and it became apparent that for him it was more important for those with him to feed on his every word, than to eat their food. He definitely desired to be the center of attention.

As I continued to listen, he told about a wild dream he had the previous night. In this dream, he walked into a room and found a lady, whom everyone at the table was acquainted with, stark naked sitting on a bed.

With his wife sitting next to him, I wondered what might be going through her mind, as he told this dream with three other ladies, perhaps his daughters, sitting at the table. I was curious as to how they would react.

I observed slight smiles across their faces, but I wondered if beneath those smiles were feelings of embarrassment and perhaps even shame, that he would so boldly and loudly relate such a dream in a public place.

Suddenly, he stopped at a point which left me almost afraid to hear what was coming next, and he began telling of another dream he had about an adventure with a crocodile. This made me ponder why he suddenly changed horses in the middle of the stream.

Had he reached a place in this first dream experience that even he felt a tinge of guilt about? Is this where he drew the line? I sensed he was disappointed at the response he was receiving in telling the dream about the crocodile, as he changed the subject to a recent travel adventure.

He began speaking about how he made a person, who has the same name as a well-known celebrity, do things that were far below their dignity. Nothing naughty mind you, just things like pushing white shirt sleeves up and getting their hands dirty.

Then he ended the story with how cleverly he disconnected a speedometer, then reconnected it on a rental vehicle, thus cheating the rental company out of money, as they charged by the mileage used.

By now, I thought I was in tune with the way this individual was thinking. I was feeling that deep down in his soul, he had yet to make an impression on those sitting at the table. This was frustrating him to no end.

I wondered what he would do next, as I knew his hunger for recognition was not satisfied. He reached in his pocket and pulled out a handful of paper money and held them in the air, peeling them back one by one as if he was counting them.

This seemed to get the attention of those at his table, but when his wife made a comment which I could not discern, as she spoke in a soft low voice, he got mad and put it back in his pocket. Then he practically shouted, "No, this is my spending money, use your own, you are lucky I bought you a meal with it!"

Needless to say, this did not make the impression he was seeking. Shortly thereafter they left the table.

By this time, my wife and I had finished our meal and were ready to leave. As we got in our car, we noticed him walking from a nearby convenience store. He was looking at something in his hand. My wife, who had not made a single comment concerning this man while we were in the restaurant, said to me, "There he goes with his lottery tickets."

Since she had remained silent while I was observing this man while we were eating, I wondered how much of the conversation she had heard. Did he say at some point that he was going to buy lottery tickets? Perhaps while I was getting dessert?

I wondered, as he was too far away to really determine that they were lottery tickets. Strange I suppose, but I never asked my wife how she knew they were lottery tickets, for at that moment, I was feeling a lot of pain for that man. I reckon this was his final attempt to make that impression he so wanted to make with his family.

In closing, permit me to make a few things very clear. I sincerely believe that my observations of this individual were not an invasion of his privacy. We were in a public place, and he was determined to make an impression on someone, even if it had to be me.

Also, I would encourage you to take advantage of every opportunity to observe the lives of others, if you can do so without invading their privacy. How else will we ever learn to love and have feelings for those who are not the same in nature as we are, and who have needs much different than our own?

Human beings are the most interesting creatures on Earth. I have read that the greatest need expressed by human hearts, besides love, is the need of recognition, to be recognized, to make an impression.

This man made an impression that day, at least on me. An impression which left me with a new understanding of how important it is for us to make an impression on others. And to what extent a person will go to leave their "footprints in the sand."

126

The Day Camp Child

Who is this stranger? This lady who picks me up from this day camp and takes me home each night. This one who puts me in my night clothes, then to bed as she turns out the light. She wants me to call her mommy, I wonder what can that term mean? Perhaps it is someone you know who is seldom ever seen. She wakes me every morning. Then puts me in her car. Doesn't say where we're going. But when we get there I know where we are. We are in that day camp, where I spend my time. Spend my time…my time.

Left at my appointed room, others soon arrive. Then we all make our voices heard to let them know we are alive. The keeper gives us a bottle of milk which we hold upside down. It really doesn't fill our tummies, while in milk we almost drown. I would try to get her to help me, yet hopeless I found out. To get her attention, as loud as she can shout. She shouts at others and shouts at me, is this what older people do? It makes me feel so afraid but she doesn't have a clue. She doesn't have a clue…not even a clue.

There is something in my diaper, you would think the keeper would know. As I have laid here for hours and the odor has filled the room. I have screamed in this bed and my face has turned red, my how I wish I could sleep. Why have I been stuck in a room with more than this keeper can keep? Too many mouths to feed, too many bottoms to clean, too many things left undone. Gosh, oh gee, how silly of me, to wish I was the only one. I was the only one…the only one.

The keeper has come to clean me up, I guess it's closing time. The stranger will come and tell me, I had a wonderful day. The keeper will agree with her, and she will get her pay. They both smile and talk awhile, then the stranger takes me to her home. She feeds me, tells me she needs me, then puts me in my bed. She turns out the light, says goodnight, and tells me there are sugar plums dancing in my head. Sugar plums dancing in my head…sugar plums dancing.

127

All in a Day of Dieting

It is Monday. This is the day you're going to stick to it like glue. You had your binge over the weekend, knowing Monday, the big D-day, was coming. Now, it's off to war, let the battle begin.

Dressed for battle, you get in your car and drive to the nearest fast food place to get your spouse a biscuit and jelly to go with that hot cup of coffee. But none for you, you're tough. Besides, you have ammunition at home waiting for you—those dog biscuits, (oops!) I mean granola bars.

"They are good," you keep saying, and you vow to keep saying it until you believe it. However, something in the area of your brain seems to be distorting your thinking. Instead of the one biscuit with jelly you intended to order for your spouse, you order three biscuits with jelly.

Quickly you dispose of the biscuits, wiping the jelly off your lips, before getting back home. You proudly hand your spouse the biscuit and jelly, and announce you're eating those diet bars. "They're good!" you say to your spouse, who is wondering if you have lost your once very active taste buds.

Now all you need to do is make it until lunch, where that can of diet chocolate drink awaits. Your brain suddenly becomes artistic, drawing pictures of every kind of dessert you would die for. Perhaps watching television would help clear your mind. You turn it on just in time to watch that popular show, "Mr. Food." Thinking a magazine would be better, you flip the pages trying to find one that doesn't have a delicious morsel on it, but none can be found.

An early lunch sounds good at the moment, but then you discover you have suffered a severe memory loss. You go to the kitchen to get your diet drink and find that one of the six cans are missing. Since you are the only one home, and there is an empty can sitting on the counter, you must have had your diet drink and forgotten that you drank it.

"That one shouldn't count," you say to yourself and go ahead and open another. Two hours before lunch time, you drink your "mid morning snack," or at least that's what you now call it, convinced there are too many hours between breakfast and lunch to not have something between.

Still feeling good about yourself, you make it till noon, and decide a salad wouldn't be harmful to go with that diet drink. But what's a salad without a little meat? Being the good warrior you are by staying away from fried foods, you bake a chicken, and toss a few chicken legs and a chicken breast on your salad.

Feeling a little guilty about your diet lunch, you decide it's time to do that exercise you included in your diet plan. You take a walk to your bedroom where the bed is begging you to lay down for a nap. You decide that perhaps a nap would be a wise decision, as you would need to rest up for your evening exercise.

After 20 minutes or so, you keep waking up to the sound of thunder, but it's not raining outside. As you sit up in bed, you notice your stomach has learned to make the sounds of an erupting volcano. How embarrassing, you think. Perhaps digesting something light, would quiet it down. You get in your car and drive to your supermarket where light, low calorie items are everywhere. You bring home a variety of a few dozen.

Observing the expression on your face, which appears as pain from a hard day of dieting, (but in reality is the weight of guilt you are feeling) your spouse invites you out for an evening meal. "Why not?" you think.

You must show how you have fasted all day by enjoying a very large full-course dinner. Besides, your spouse could eat a two-ton truck and look like a person you're striving to be. If you don't eat a nice meal, your spouse will feel uncomfortable and this would be at the least cruel.

Just to be on the safe side, you order a few side items and insist you can have dessert since you have been so faithful to your diet all day. With your spouse feeling they have rescued you from starvation, and you feeling a little guilty but mostly full, you sink in the car seat as your spouse drives toward the house.

You tell your spouse how wonderful it was and how it could not have been better, well, except perhaps unless the two of you stopped somewhere on the way home for some cheese cake and coffee. Wanting to make this evening anything but perfect, your spouse picks up quickly on this suggestion.

When you arrive for your cheese cake you notice they specialize in ice cream also and suggest taking some home. Why spoil your evening by refusing you some ice cream, your spouse replies, as you slowly walk to car. I mean, very slowly, you walk to the car. After all, you need a walk, to work off some of this food you have been enjoying all evening. Besides, this give the ice cream time to soften up.

As you finally head for home, you inform your spouse the ice cream is leaking out, and must be consumed immediately before it ruins the seat of the car. With permission to perform this dreadful task, you dive into all three gallons, explaining why one should not eat ice cream and drive.

Home at last your spouse tells you of how proud they are of your dieting efforts, and that you were an angel to ruin it a little to save the car seats from considerable damage. "It was the least I could do," you humbly reply. After all, "It's all in a day of dieting."

Needless to say, this story is a bit exaggerated. Do we eat to live, or live to eat? After all, this is really the question. As for me, I am going to see if there is any chicken left in the fridge.

128

It's Saturday Morning

It's a beautiful Saturday morning. I am sitting on the weathered wooden planks of my back porch. The cool morning breeze is a gentle reminder that the fall season is near.

As I look toward the east, I observe the rising of that lucky old sun. It has harkened the call of a rooster who is crowing somewhere nearby. As the red brilliance of the sun rises over the muddy brown waters of the Mississippi river, I hear the sound of a train rushing down the rails which run parallel with the riverfront. The clanging sound of the train wheels, and its whistle blowing at each crossing, brings back memories of my grandfather who was once a conductor on such a train.

As I look toward the west, I see three birds perched on top of a utility pole, singing their praises to the Lord, I suppose. It must be eight o'clock, as the bells of Saint Mary's are ringing. How faithful are these bells each morning. The church, which is in full view as I look toward the south, is one of the great landmarks in my neighborhood. It has been a historic symbol which has brought back many memories of my past back to life.

The funeral home which is in the path between the church and my house, is now a daily reminder that life on this earth is but temporal, and the church is a daily reminder that for those who trust in God, life is eternal.

129

My Perceptions

Was my perception wrong,
Were my feelings just deceived.
Were my standards set to high,
For the things which I believed.

Was I asking far too much,
From my sisters and my brothers.
To be treated with the same,
That I had gave to others.

It must have been a fantasy,
Things read between the lines.
To think that I was a single rose,
Amongst a field of dandelions.

What made me think that I was different,
That I alone was right.
That I could change the heart of man,
And make everything look bright.

That I could add the beauty,
To an ugly world of sin.
Me, oh my, how foolish,
I have surely been.

It must have been a fantasy,
Things read between the lines.

To think that I was a single rose,
Amongst a field of dandelions.

130

I'll See You in My Dreams

I have never been one to like goodbyes, and I do not accept the notion that all good things must come to an end. Nevertheless, I am aware of a truth which was recently pointed out to me in a general conversation. That truth being, "Everything has a price."

If you want to take on a new project which requires your time, there will be something you will no longer be able to give time to. For time is a precious gift we receive to use as we see fit. The way we use our time determines the quality of the life we have lived.

I have said all that to say this: This will be my last column in TBY. I have been writing this column, which had its beginnings in the "Current Local" in Van Buren, for more than five years. It was inspired by author Marjorie Holmes, and has been supported by my readers who have been the best audience anyone could ask for.

I have enjoyed writing this column more than you could begin to imagine, it has been the joy of my life.

Now I must move onto other things I feel the Lord has directed me to do. We are living in a time of extreme importance and at least for myself, I feel called to make these last days the most valuable days I have to give and share with others, divided with fellowship, and covered with love.

I hope you enjoy the analogy of the Grand Canyon and grandchildren. My grandson is five years old, which kind of dates this story. It was one of the first articles I had in the Van Buren newspaper and will be my last article in TBY.

The Grand Canyon and Grandchildren

Have you ever gone to visit someone who had just come back from the Grand Canyon? If so, you probably watched slides and looked at dozens, if not a hundred, pictures of one of the most beautiful wonders of the world.

265

If you have ever been in the same room with a parent who had just become a grandparent, you probably were asked to look at Grandma and Grandpa's brag book photo album of one of the most beautiful wonders of the world. As I tried to feel as excited about their trip to the Grand Canyon or as joyful as they were over the new addition to the family, of this I was certain, some things cannot be conveyed in conversation. They must be experienced in a more personal way.

I had heard about the Grand Canyon for decades. For me it was one of the wonders of the world that I would see pictures of, and hear people talk about, people who had been there (which seemed like everyone but me).

I would never have believed that the day would come when I would be standing on the floor of one of its lookout spots and admiring all of its beauty. Regardless of who is telling you about it, or how much you want to be there, you cannot appreciate it unless you have experienced the trip yourself.

I also had heard about grandchildren for decades. For me, they were one of the wonders of the world that I would see pictures of and hear people talk about, people who had grandchildren (which seemed like everyone but me). I would never have believed that the day would come when I would be standing on the floor of one of its look-in spots and admiring all of its beauty. Being a grandparent is a life experience. Regardless of who is telling you about it, or how much you want to be one, you cannot appreciate the honor until you have become one. Does this sound familiar?

The similarity of the breathtaking beauty of the Grand Canyon and grandchildren are remarkable. When my wife and I arrive at the Grand Canyon, she had that look on her face that said, "I never thought I would live to experience this." She had that same look on her face as she came down the hall with the doctor and said to me, "Come, look at our grandson."

While at the Grand Canyon we used four or five rolls of film, taking more pictures than the previous three years had generated. When our grandchild made his grand entrance into the world, we bought a VCR camera and make a 60 minute video, starring our grandchild, in the first two days at the hospital.

When you're at the Grand Canyon, depending on the time of day and the overcast, you feel as if it is has many faces. This is due to the many formations and colors of the rocks. Each time, you see a face you have not noticed before. You sound like someone at a Fourth of July picnic who's watching a firework display. As each scene gets better, the sound from your lips gets louder.

Is this also true with a grandchild, you may ask? You must be kidding. We were standing on our heads, trying to get an expression this kid had not already made or that we had on film. Every time he wrinkled his nose, yawned or sneezed, we would say, "Quick, get the camera." And I don't care what they say about him "just passing gas," he smiled at me because he loved his Grandpa.

Grand Canyon or grandchildren, every new observation you make becomes a Kodak moment. If you have been to the Grand Canyon and you're waiting to become a grandparent, or if you are a grandparent waiting to go to the Grand Canyon, perhaps this comparison will help you know what to expect.

If you have not had the opportunity to enjoy either of these events, there are no words I can say that will permit you to feel what I felt. All I can say is to pray to the Almighty that he will bless you with both of these blessings, and remember to take your camera, for every moment is a Kodak moment with the Grand Canyon and grandchildren.

131

How Many Years Can a Night Last?

How many years can a night last?
I've seen every crack in the floor.
I've looked at the phone at least a million times,
And listened for the knock at my door.

With a book as my only companion,
The pages get worn out so fast.
Are you hearing my plea, would someone please tell me,
How many years can a night last.

Well the night is so long, if I was right or wrong,
I'd lose every fight with myself.
I'd be too tired to look, at every single book,
That I took a bed and put back on the shelf.

How many years can a night last?
How long at the ceiling can I stare.
Well I'm doing time with old letters that I find,
From friends who no longer seem to care.

Spending a night with my memories,
surrounded completely by the past.
Are you hearing my plea, would someone please tell me,
How many years can a night last.

Are you hearing my plea, would someone please tell me,
How many years can a night last.